ORIGINAL PEACE

Restoring God's Creation

David Burrell, C.S.C., *and* Elena Malits, C.S.C.

PAULIST PRESS
New York / Mahwah, N.J.

This book is printed on recycled paper.

Cover Art: "The Peaceable Kingdom" by Edward Hicks, American (1780–1849), courtesy Art Resource. Cover design by Morris Berman Studio.

Library of Congress Cataloging-in-Publication Data

Burrell, David B.
    Original peace : restoring God's creation / David Burrell and Elena Malits.
        p.   cm.
    ISBN 0-8091-3733-X (alk. paper)
    1. Creation. 2. Nature—Religious aspects—Christianity. 3. Peace—Religious aspects—Christianity. I. Malits, Elena. II. Title.
BT695.B78   1997
231.7′65—dc21   97-17543
                                                                                           CIP

Published by Paulist Press
997 Macarthur Boulevard
Mahwah, New Jersey 07430

Printed and bound in the
United States of America

CONTENTS

In memory of John Gerber, C.S.C.,
1930–1995
whose creative insight and redemptive presence
enlivened so many

PREFACE

This joint effort originated as a response to a request by Donald Brophy, Paulist editor, for a work attending to issues addressed by what has come to be called "creation theology"—a series of attempts to correct past distortions that have proved their currency by a notable response from readers. Yet like so many others, we too had sensed something missing in these attempts. In searching for a way to correct what might be termed a "cyclops" focus on creation, the baptismal creed with its three articles presented itself as a time-honored corrective. John Milbank's suggestion that we view redemption as "restoring God's original peace" offered a way of adroitly balancing creation and redemption, and so gave us our title. He displayed the connective tissue between these two doctrines. Our respective concerns in communicating with college students over a joint teaching span of fifty years helped both of us identify the topics for consideration. Thus began a formal collaboration in a text addressed to informed readers as free as possible from technical theological jargon.

This book is a collaborative effort by two people in agreement concerning every position stated. Each of those positions has been elaborated through hours of mutually illuminating discussion and occasionally painful disagreements. Each of us can say he or she owns every part of the text. Nonetheless, we remain two individuals whose concerns and perspectives also differ. Where the experience of one of us is paramount, the singular will be used; where our concerns merge, the plural reflects that fact.

What makes this effort truly collaborative is that we bring to it our respective expertise. If David Burrell's has become the comparative exploration of Judaism, Christianity, and Islam, Elena Malits sees hers as a mediating role, making work of that sort intelligible to nonspecialists. It was, in fact, she who insisted that we keep particular people in our mind's eye as we write—people who are deeply interested in theological questions, yet are not theologians. (It is serendipitous that as we complete these very words, we will have supper with two of them—Eva Hooker, C.S.C., from St. John's University, Collegeville, and Penny Gill from Mount Holyoke College. They did not know it, but each time David wrote a sentence that only Karl Rahner might understand, Elena screamed, "Eva and Penny would never comprehend that!")

We take joint responsibility for the final product, where vastly different work habits have at times tested a long friendship. Those travails will, we hope, make the presentation that much clearer and so facilitate the reading. Our indebtedness stretches across time and space in ways we are unable to acknowledge here all at once. But that is, of course, the fruit of years of living in community and entering into diverse communal endeavors. Although footnotes are kept to a minimum, our gratitude to one or another of our colleagues will appear as the argument unfolds. Here we must thank Don Brophy for the original suggestion, and Paulist Press staff for their patience in its protracted execution.

INTRODUCTION:
AN INTERFAITH APPROACH

The balance in question is that among the three articles of the creed: creation, redemption, and sanctification, attributed to the "persons" of Father, Son, and Spirit respectively. Yet since a balance normally seeks equipoise between two objects, it is creation and redemption we shall address. The third dimension, *sanctification,* will be effectively at work in seeking to balance the first two, since the constant appeal will be made to Christian, Muslim, and Jewish practice. So this inquiry is presented as a way of doing theology that does justice to our situation as Christians vis-à-vis other major religions. And while the focus will be the three Abrahamic faiths, one chapter will venture into *vedanta* to suggest how that faith perspective can help to clarify an issue remaining for the other three.

Our guides in this inquiry will be two theologians in Britain, Nicholas Lash and John McDade, S.J., and in particular Nicholas Lash's recent *Believing Three Ways in One God* coupled with a contemporary article by McDade.[1] Lash's strategy directs us to the creed, which he exploits in order to show the inherently trinitarian cast of Christian faith by taking each article in turn, and using the others to comment on it. McDade responds to ecological concerns by showing how a theology fully responsive to Christian revelation requires a dual focus: creation plus redemption. Yet the second article of the creed—the mini-narrative of redemption—has so eclipsed the others in the outworking of Christian theology that an expressly interfaith perspective will be useful to restore the balance with creation. The proof is in the pudding, of course, so readers will have to assess how useful this strategy will be. Turning to the Qur'an to illustrate a point in Christian faith will doubtless seem forced to many, but those who have lived in any proximity with persons of another faith will find such a conversation quite natural.

It is part of the persuasive argument of this work that conversations like these will become more frequent, and are already beginning to create a new context for theology. And if some may find them threatening, the burden of this inquiry is to show rather how fruitful they can be. The new setting for Christian faith that Karl Rahner sketched out in 1979 has in fact come to be. And the suggestion is that rather than dilute that inquiry, comparative considerations can help to restore imbalances and discover new perspectives for elaborating revelation. In this case, it can be said that nothing short of a Keplerian revolution is called for in Christian theology. For the key to Copernicus's strategy to rethink the earth and planets as a solar system rather than a geosystem spinning about the earth as its center was being able to think of earth and planets alike as following not circular but elliptical paths. What stood in the way of this very conception was Aristotle's conviction that perfect motion was circular motion, and that the heavens had to exhibit perfection. Yet the facts spoke otherwise, as empirical observations traced an elliptical path for all the planets as well as the earth once the sun assumed its central place. And ellipses are constituted by twin foci, as anyone can verify with a piece of string and two pegs. It was Kepler's proposal to replace Aristotle's predilection for perfect circles with the geometric configuration of an ellipse that allowed Copernicus's revolution in our vision of the heavens to win the day.

What is interesting for our inquiry, however, is the energy generated *between* these two centers: how a focus on creation can reveal Jesus' mission to be one intent on restoring the original order of God's creation, while the ways in which that order had been undermined by human sin required the suffering and death of the Son of Man for its restoration. So redemption is modeled on creation, yet that original order will continue to escape us without the restorative, indeed the re-creating activity of redemption. For it is certainly the same God who creates and redeems, and if we use two different terms to denote two distinct divine activities, that is only because the ensuing disorder required a fresh response. An interfaith perspective will help us to see these two activities as reflecting a single divine plan, and so restore the works attributed to Father, Son, and Spirit as those of one God whose loving initiative sustains us in being as well as offers us the capacity for responding to that sustenance as providential care. For both Islam and Judaism see God's revelation and covenant as continuous with the gratuitous act of creating all-that-is "from nothing," that is, as an act of sovereign divine freedom that testifies to creation as "all grace." We shall see how this perspective helps to restore Christian theology and especially the doctrine of a triune God to its inherent balance.

We shall carry out this exploration in stages, beginning with some reflections on the place and destiny of human beings in God's creation. An age of ecological awareness has taken umbrage at the biblical perspective, which purports to place human beings above the rest of creation, especially in the light of the Lord God's directive to "subdue" the earth, interpreted in modern times as license to exploit the earth as a resource for human endeavors. Reacting to that misreading of Genesis, some contemporary Christian proponents have sought to restore a holistic perspective by seeking a "new story" that accents cosmic emergence, while minimizing the particularity of God's revelation in Jesus with its attendant story of sin and redemption. Following our master metaphor of an ellipse with twin foci, we sketch an alternative picture of Jesus' mission as one of restoring the original peace of God's gratuitous creation, showing why "the Christ had to suffer and so enter into his glory" in order to consummate that very call. This novel yet quite traditional reading of "the atonement" leads us to a fresh perspective on human suffering and death, with some assistance from Buddhist teaching on the quenching of desire.

Returning to a more conventional outline of the life of Christians, we consider in turn the seven canonical sacraments, showing how church practice contains a great potential to link people of faith with the larger gift of God's free creation. From that explicitly Christian, indeed ecclesial, narrative, we ask what mutual light Muslim and Christian practice can train on the way in which human beings can effectively participate in the mission of restoring the original order of God's creation. These reflections on "grace" then lead us to mine the resources of a Christian contemplative who has made her home in the Indian subcontinent, to help us utilize the initially puzzling notion of *nonduality* to shed light on the effort of those traditions that focus on creation to articulate the relation of divinity to the universe. Finally, we shall offer some indications of how this dual perspective of a Christian faith rooted in the free gifts of creation and of redemption alters the ultimate horizons of the life of the universe and our life, which theological jargon refers to by the formidable name of *eschatology*. Paul's teaching that "as all die in Adam so all will be made alive in Christ"(1 Cor 15:22) certainly implies his doctrine of "original sin," yet it does not turn uniquely on the human-centered features of his thought. A creation that is freely given can also be graciously transformed. If the death that humans associate with Adam appears to us as a punishment for transgression, the fact remains that death itself is quite natural to all of God's creation. Indeed, it is the precondition, as we shall see, for the life that ends in death to be transformed into a new kind of life "in Christ." Exploring the continuities and discontinuities of that transformation with life as we find it in creation will complete our inquiry.

1

HUMANS' PLACE IN GOD'S CREATION

Jewish, Christian, and Muslim scriptures invite us to hear and accept that the universe is freely created by one God who cares for it and offers human beings a special role to play in its development. Both the Bible and the Qur'an have something to *say* about that special role. Even more fundamental, however, is the fact that human beings constitute the only portion of the universe able to *hear* what these scriptures proclaim about everything being freely created. Indeed, that capacity singles us out and portends human destiny.

We need to be told that the universe is created freely by God, but the very capacity to recognize that "fact" already implies what we human beings are to do with our lives. For if all-that-is comes to us as *gift,* then a commensurate response must be elicited from those who receive it. And in this case the response should be no less than total, since what has been received is not *something* but *everything,* including the being of the conscious recipient. So those who can hear that creation is God's free gift are already set off from the rest of the universe that is not so addressed. Only human beings are able to respond or fail to respond. Other creatures may be said to "return" the gift by fulfilling their respective natures, but that can be deemed only a metaphorical way of speaking.

From the perspective of the revelation of creation as a free gift, then, human beings are not so much *set apart* by an explicit and deliberate act of the creator, as the capacity to hear and to

7

respond to this news already sets us apart. (The same holds, of course, for those proponents of "deep ecology" whose *theories* assert that there is no specific difference between humans and the rest of creation—except the capacity to formulate such theories!) Ironically enough, as we shall see, the divine revelation concerning God's singular activity of freely creating the universe will not so much exalt human beings to a posture of arrogant superiority as require us to render a peculiar service to the universe. That service is, in fact, an integral part of the response we owe God for being able to recognize our very existence as a divine gift. But human response is wayward. We are familiar with unbelievers and believers alike taking biblical or Qur'anic words out of context to satisfy human desires. It may prove illuminating, therefore, to see how the full picture offered by the Bible or the Qur'an radically alters the account of human specificity—and does so in the direction of wholehearted respect and gratitude for creation.

Among the three traditions that aver free creation, the Qur'an has the simplest presentation, so let us begin with the place and destiny of human beings in God's creation from the perspective of Islamic revelation. For Muslims, God is first and last creator; everything follows from that assertion. Human beings, however, could not know what sort of a creator this is except that God tell us. To accept that God is creator and has made it known to human beings is, therefore, precisely what identifies the believer. By contrast, the unbeliever rejects God as creator and revealer of being creator: "We created not the heavens and the earth and all that is between them in vain. That is the opinion of those who disbelieve" (38:27, cf. 3:191). Through God's revelation and the believer's acceptance of it, then, the divine purpose is accomplished: "Deem you then that We had created you for nothing, and that you would not be returned to Us" (23:115). Moreover, by the very act of believing the believer is involved in the way in which the divine purpose is accomplished. For if God is revealed as creator precisely by acting so as to tell us about it, then to become a believer is to give thanks spontaneously for the Qur'an. And that can only be a wholehearted response to the gift of creation.

In fact, *islam* means "a submission in love and obedience of one's whole life to God as creator, provider, and final end of mankind," so the very term itself points to a capacity for wholehearted response as what sets human beings off from the rest of creation.[1] In the Qur'anic narrative we accept God's gift of *trust,* but then do as we wish. The creator says: "We offered the trust *[amâ-nah]* to the heavens and the earth, and to the mountains, but they shrank from bearing it and were afraid of it. And man assumed it. Lo! he has proved a tyrant *[zalûm]* and a fool *[jahûl]*" (33:72). To accept the trust yet not carry it out is a plausible story regarding human conduct. Proposing a primordial covenant, however, offers a picture of what we are committed to by the mere recognition of our origins. (There are two other words in the Qur'an that can be rendered "covenant": *'ahd* and *mithâq,* yet the notion of covenant is far less central to the Qur'an than to the Hebrew scriptures. This could be so because the Qur'an is neither directed to nor preoccupied with a single people, but to human beings as such, so a historical convenant could not figure in its outworking.)

Human beings are free, of course, to acknowledge the *trust* or to avoid it. The normal human situation is deemed to be avoidance, identified in the Islamic tradition as *jâhiliyya* or ignorance. It is this situation that the revelation is given to rectify. It does so by informing us of an ordered chain: "creation-preservation-guidance-judgment, all as manifestations of [divine] mercy."[2] And the beginning and end of this chain—God's role as creator and as judge—mutually corroborate each other. The One who brought all-that-is out of nothing would have no difficulty restoring all persons to life on the last day to face judgment regarding their acquittal of the trust.[3]

What makes the Qur'anic account of the dignity and foolishness of human beings simpler than the Hebrew scriptures, in either their Jewish or Christian readings, is the absence of any theme of *redemption.* There is, nonetheless, plenty said about

evil in the Qur'an; in Islamic tradition the notion of *jâhiliyya*
functions as a virtual analogue to the Christian doctrine of "original sin," despite the protests of Muslims that they have no such
teaching. Of course they are correct to insist (as Jews do as well)
that they have no elaboration of the original man and woman
story to match that of Paul. Indeed, the "salvation history" analogue in Sura 2 dispatches the matter in three verses *[ayât]:*

> And We said: O Adam! You and your wife dwell in the garden,
> and eat freely [of the fruits] there where you will; but come not
> near this tree lest you become wrongdoers. (35) But Satan caused
> them to deflect therefrom and expelled them from the [happy]
> state in which they were; and we said: Fall down [all of you], each
> of you a foe to the other!...(36) Then Adam received from his
> Lord words [of revelation] and He relented towards him. Lo! He
> is the Relenting, the Merciful. (37)

God's forgiveness on the spot clearly obviates the need for a
redeemer. So while the episode offers an etiology for human sinfulness (the phrase "all of you" envisages Adam's descendants), it dra-
matizes God's forgiving mercy much more than human sinfulness.

This emphasis allows the Qur'an to insist that the "creation of
the world and of human beings remains the first and paramount
sign of [God's] unique compassion: God need not have created
the world at all, [yet] would still have remained utterly just and
generous in so doing."[4] The triptych of compassion, justice, and
generosity—all names of God—cannot simply be inferred from
the world as we might examine it, but derives solely from God's
correlatively compassionate act of revealing to humankind the
"straight path" of the Qur'an (cf. 1:6).[5] Given this understanding
of the world and our place in it, the only reasonable response on
our part is to return it all to God.

For the most part, however, we do not carry through on that.
Islam may indeed be a most "rational" religion, as some recent
apologetic strategies would have it, but human beings are often less

than rational. So what can move us beyond our own interests to respond commensurately to such a revelation? Surely not fear of an adverse judgment at the end of time. Love is best elicited by the manifest love of the other. Is this evident in Islam? Muslims argue that the Qur'an states it, while the very gift of the Qur'an shows it. But is that enough? What seems to be wanting in Islam is precisely the manifestation of a Father's love as displayed so dramatically in the life, death, and resurrection of Jesus "so that the disperse children of God may be gathered into one" (Jn 11:52). That love is especially poignant when understood in the light of God's plaintive appeal to the people of Israel: "I will make...an everlasting covenant with them..., my dwelling place shall be with them; I will be their God, and they shall be my people. Then the nations shall know that I the Lord sanctify Israel" (Ez 37: 26–28).

For Muslims, however, what apparently offers the most tangible witness to God's loving care is the community itself, the *umma.* Here is where people learn to pray and to follow the mores that have been prescribed for life among Muslims since the earliest days in Medina. The spirit of that initial time is preserved in the *hadiths,* which offer a living testimony to the Prophet's response to diverse situations. Indeed, the *umma* sees itself as a created reflection of the Qur'an to offer human beings the way to respond as creatures to their creator. Thus we are reminded that however rational a wholehearted response to the creator may be, it will never be carried out except with the assistance of others and the élan provided by living witnesses. Here the relationship between master and disciple (or *pir* and *murid*), celebrated in Sufi circles, offers the clearest example of such a bonding, while Christians see something similar among older and younger members within religious orders.

We must, indeed, ask how the image of the original gift of creation can sustain and shape the life and worship of all believing communities. It is possible to imagine ways in which they could be oriented explicitly to renewing the earth and its resources. Yet that is not the ordinary implication of *islam,* nor does it shape the agenda of Christian communities in general or religious orders in particular. Traditionally the latter have been completely absorbed in becoming "followers of Jesus" rather than "children of a gracious creator." Neither in contemplative nor in active orders have men and women thought of their communities as schools for learning how to return everything to their creator. At best there has been some stress on following Jesus to worship "the Father." But the connection between "Father" and "creator" has not been obvious to Christians, even though the creed makes it explicit. Nonetheless, among members of religious orders, even if not consciously grasped, the connection between Father and creator has been displayed in practice, notably in the practice of devoting time and energy to promoting a full range of those educational and healing endeavors we call "culture." The historical link between religious orders and culture should remind us that "creation" includes human endeavors as well as the world of nature. Both emanate from the hand of the creator, if indeed in different ways. Culture involves human creativity, whose roots lie in the creator's initiative. Benedict's maxim, *ora et labora*—pray and work, captures the way in which Christian communities quite naturally turn to using the gifts of their members to return those same gifts to the creator—at a profit, as the Gospel commends (Mt 25:14–30).

What is fascinating about this link between religious orders and culture is its very spontaneity, and the way it characterizes communities without any apparent justification. To the query why one spends time on such "secular" pursuits, often there is no articulate response except the Western pragmatic one: We ought to be doing something useful. Indeed, the inner connection between prayer and work, redemption and creation, is less than obvious. Perhaps a closer look at the mission of Jesus from the perspective we have been suggesting will illuminate the relationships involved.

2

THE MISSION OF JESUS

The organization of the traditional Christian creeds into three distinct articles—the Father as creator, the Son as redeemer, and the Spirit as sanctifier—does not invite us to focus on the mission of the Son with respect to creation. The Nicene creed, however, makes an explicit declaration. In the second article, after speaking of the eternal generation of the Son but before riveting our attention on his salvific work, we find this assertion concerning the only begotten Son of God: "Through him all things were made." So the Son is said to have a mission prior to that of being savior— namely, to be the one through whom all things were created. Since creation is a free act of God, this statement has to refer to a mission and not to the Son's eternal emanation. Yet there is an entirely coherent correspondence between them; as Aquinas remarks, the emanation of all things from the creator follows the pattern of the eternal emanation of the Son within God (ST 1.45.6). He cites Anselm approvingly: "By uttering Himself the Father uttered all creatures" (*De Veritate* [On Truth] 4.4, *Monologion* 33). These remarks alert us to see the Son's mission of salvation in the light of his prior role of being the one through whom all-that-is comes to be. In short, it is the Son who is to be our savior precisely because he is sent to restore the original order of creation which he himself constitutes. John Milbank calls this initial order "God's original peace," alluding to the startling discrepancy between the biblical accounts of creation and their Babylonian antecedents.[1]

Several passages in the New Testament support the thesis that the savior comes to restore the order of creation. Wanting to establish a norm for marriage that was expressly at variance with the Mosaic code, Jesus appealed to what prevailed "in the beginning" (Mt 19:8, Mk 10:6). Matthew invokes Psalm 78:2 as an editorial comment on Jesus' practice of teaching in parables that "expound things hidden since the foundation of the world" (Mt 13:35).[2] The prologue of John inextricably weaves together Christ's mission of salvation with that of creation; one might even argue that it gives precedence to the latter: "Through him all things came to be, not one thing had its being but through him" (1:3). But it is Ephesians that is most explicit: "Blessed be the God and Father of our Lord Jesus Christ, who…has made known to us in all wisdom and insight the mystery of his will, according to his purpose which he set forth in Christ as a plan for the fullness of time, to unite all things in him, things in heaven and things on earth" (1:3, 9–10). "To unite all things in him" goes right to the point of Jesus' mission. And when this statement from Ephesians is linked with the fourth gospel's insistence that "through him all things came to be," then the epistle's paeans to the cosmic Christ are removed from the realm of rhetoric to that of sober theological discourse.

Moreover, this same "God and Father…has blessed us in Christ with every spiritual blessing in the heavenly places, even as he chose us in him before the foundation of the world" (Eph 1:3–4). The decisive "before" in this passage alludes to our share in Christ's mission to restore the original order of things. For to be chosen in Christ *before* his mission of constituting all of creation is to give human beings a way of sharing in that mission that bespeaks an intimacy even greater than that which the entire universe has to its order. It places us "beside him, like a master craftsman," inviting us to appropriate to ourselves—by virtue of having been chosen "in him"—all that Proverbs 8:22–31 says of God's wisdom.

So what sets off human beings from the rest of creation hardly alienates us from it, but rather unites us with that very One who constitutes its inherent order. The second article of the creed will remind us what union with Christ in that restorative mission will entail. And we should expect nothing less, given the disorder that prevails in the world we know. Anyone seeking to restore the "original peace of creation" faces an insurmountable task. As the gospels never cease to remind us, that was true of Jesus. Nothing he could *do*—from "teaching with authority" to "casting out demons" (Lk 4:36, 9:6)—would be able to rectify the situation. The disorder into which the universe had fallen could not simply be *fixed,* not even by the very one through whom it was constituted! What stands in the way is the superhuman power of human sin, daunting even the creator of all. Sin can be acknowledged only by those who perpetrate it and then present themselves, along with what they have done, for forgiveness. And forgiveness presumes, indeed demands, that the sinner accept responsibility for the deed.

The primordial narrative of Genesis 3 is instructive regarding how sin establishes itself as a pervasive disorder through human denial of responsibility. It can better be read as a story of "original sin" if we focus not on the transgression itself but on its aftermath. Both the man and the woman deny that they are at fault. They were but responding to the bidding of another: the man to the woman, the woman to the snake. Neither claims that he or she is accountable for transgressing a divine command; each protests that someone or something else is to blame. No one is simply able to say, "Yes, I did what I knew I was not supposed to do." In a few short verses, the story shows how the persistent avoidance of responsibility is what constitutes the organized disorder of sin. We need not read on very far in the Genesis text to learn how the world then becomes a complex network of human denial and deceit. And nobody will accept responsibility for the bloody mess! Human beings attempt to deceive not only God, but themselves.

Herbert Fingarette's analysis of self-deception offers a prescient image for this dimension of sin, which allows us to sin without acknowledging that we have done so. We avoid calling actions by their proper names, and so by engaging in the language of cover-up we manage to talk ourselves into doing what we otherwise know is wrong. All the while, this evasive language completes the charade and confirms the deception.[3] What Fingarette takes pains to analyze is a simple maneuver known intimately to us all: No one sets out to commit adultery; we rather find ourselves in a situation where we cannot resist enjoying another's presence. Slang expressions embody this maneuver cagily: No one *steals* from a supermarket; they "rip something off," or even "liberate it." Any action that requires language to go through such labored contortions to carry it through deserves what Bernard Lonergan calls it: "the surd of sin."[4] And Lonergan is simply illustrating the observation of Augustine that deliberate evil could never represent a positive increment in being, but always denotes that something specific is *missing*.[5] This view of evil as *privation* may at first appear unduly "metaphysical," but when we realize what we must do with language in planning or in recounting evil, it is confirmed. That is why we find certain transgressions, like assassination, especially horrendous: The one who was killed meant so much to so many! (In that case, we even countenance a special term to denote such an act of murder, a term applied when the victim holds a crucial public role.) Similarly, the *privative* character of evil emerges in Israel when "Holocaust Day" comes around: We can hardly say that we *celebrate* such an event; at best we mark it or observe it.

Perhaps we can begin to appreciate the "necessity" of Jesus' suffering and death: why it was "necessary that the Christ should suffer these things and enter into his glory," as well as why we are so "slow of heart to believe all that the prophets have spoken"

(Lk 24:25). For prophets are sent to unveil the truth, while we are ensconced in the "big lie" of self-deception, pursuing success in a disordered world. This situation can be unmasked only in the measure that we are brought to realize that the prevailing practices of our lives can pointedly bring about the death of the sinless one.[6] For Jesus to fulfill his mission of restoring the order of creation, a way had to be found to bring us—collectively and individually—to our senses. As we have noted, nothing could undo the pervasive disorder of sin but repentance. Yet repentance presupposes acknowledgment, while everything in the pervasive disorder militates against acknowledging that it is a disorder! There is too much at stake in maintaining the charade. So it is hardly strange that the symbol of the crucifix is so central to Christianity, yet also understandable how easily it can become domesticated. For the pull of "the world" is nearly irresistible as we allow the expectations of others to set our goals. Taking our bearings from "the crucified one" would seem to defy the very environment that sustains us.

This hard truth probably explains the impulse in Christianity to create alternative environments to "the world" by forming communities of persons intentionally seeking to follow Jesus. Yet these communities have not been explicitly focused on the mission of Jesus as restoring the original order of creation. Since Jesus' mission has normally been formulated in anthropocentric terms, the image of the "kingdom of God" was bound to suggest a call to the transformation of human beings. Nonetheless, the disorder that sin introduces into the universe pervades every corner of it. Indeed, as we have recently become aware, much of what might be called "natural evil" now bears the stamp of human rapacity. So those who monitor world hunger remind us how deeply the roots of famine are mired in political callousness.[7] In effect, the call to those who would "restore all things in Christ" must now be to an ecological consciousness. Nothing short of that can do justice to participation in Jesus' mission of restoring God's original peace.

If we ask ourselves why such a perspective on the mission of Jesus should appear to us at this point in history, a complex cultural analysis is called for. One could argue that until quite recently, agrarian societies still shared in the ecological consciousness that had characterized hunting-gathering societies. Indeed, that very consciousness was a condition for the survival of agrarian societies. Consider how the Azande, rice farmers in East Bengal, have related to the elements of nature on which they are so dependent. Their practices amount to a folk wisdom regarding planting and harvesting. Lacking the ability to make any large-scale changes, they needed to live and work with nature in the most fruitful harmony possible. In an article challenging any wholesale application of the "secularization thesis," Peter Winch pondered the attitude of cultivators like these toward traditional rituals in the face of imported fertilizers. To the surprise of Western observers, traditional farmers utilized both.[8] (Such practices would not immediately disconfirm the "secularization thesis," of course, since its proponents could always advise that we wait a generation or two.) Winch wanted us to learn from the situation that these farmers understood something that Western capitalists did not. They perceived, it seems, that while technological advances offered another kind of help, fertilizers could not supply them with a way of relating to their life and to their work. Nor could they assure any regularity to the larger rhythms of wind, sun, and rain. If we acknowledge both of these to be framing contexts of our life and work, it should be clear that each lies beyond human control: Our root attitudes are seldom reflected upon, and the cosmic patterns are too vast for us to comprehend. By their actions the peasants were saying: Trust in your fertilizers if you will, but we know that agriculture is much more than a "means of production"; it is also a way of life for us.

Like the Westerners in this illustration, it may well be that we are the ones who cannot grasp the implications of our faith in cosmic terms, whereas earlier Christians could. Agrarian societies were alert to incorporating traditional modes of interaction with the earth into their expressions of faith—think of the various blessings, seasonal processions, and ceremonies focused on elements in nature. Rhythms of sacred time may not all have been derived from nature, yet religious rituals of the community nearly always included the rhythms of nature itself. Patristic commentaries on the patterns of salvific action exploit these connections explicitly. Indeed, this is so much the case with regard to Easter and spring that someone formed by that literature might wonder how the paschal season could even be celebrated in the southern hemisphere! Agrarian societies found incorporating seasonal patterns into religious ritual to be both natural to everyday life and enhancing for believers. By contrast, urban industrial society tends to regard the processes of nature marginal, and such ritual practices "unproductive." And what is deemed unproductive is at worst meaningless and at best irrelevant. As Gerard Manley Hopkins put it: "Nor can foot feel/being shod." The coincidence of Vatican II liturgical reforms with a turn to anthropological concerns led many theologians whose thinking was congruent with urban industrial society to question the relevance of blessings and other ecclesial practices that have come to be called "sacramentals."[9] In retrospect, these theologians might have been better advised to engage in a more trenchant critique of their own cultural presuppositions and to remember the old adage that it is more sensible to acknowledge that what we may simply not understand we are prone to call silly.

This nearly exclusive preoccupation of the churches with the human dimension of creation has led some astute critics to call for a "new story" that substitutes "cosmic emergence" for the familiar drama of sin and redemption.[10] The strategy recommended here, however, does not substitute one perspective for another, but rather invites one to explore the dialectical tension between creation and redemption. We have approached them as twin foci of revelation, as in the first two articles of the creed.

And while we need to move beyond a purely anthropocentric focus to include the earth, we must not forget that culture is part of God's creation as well. Current views of freedom as *autonomy* could tempt us to remove human actions, capable of evil, from the ambit of God's creation—at once to preserve divine justice and to safeguard human freedom.[11] Yet the human dimension of creation remains within God's overall providential intent, and to exclude it romanticizes creation in its natural state while denying culture the status of being created by God. An anthropological focus accentuates the distinction of culture from nature, but that is not the only way to relate one to the other. "Creation" can be understood as gathering up all that is—nature and culture, natural and supernatural—into one immense gift, albeit a gift we have spurned and spoiled so that it needs to be restored. The hubris of human attempts to master and to dominate nature spawned a romantic reaction that presumed that natural and cultural energies had to be opposed to one another. It is precisely this presumption that every effort to raise ecological consciousness must counter by showing how closely our destiny is linked to sane ecological policies. The bifurcation of creation into nature and culture has helped to countenance policies that, again, simply presume that short-term efficiencies must characterize human endeavor, while any other perspective is dubbed "romantic."

Perhaps nothing short of a theology that sees all activity in this world as also the action of God—even more intimately than it is that of the human agent—can overcome the mindset that opposes culture to nature.[12] In any case, we are contending that the same God who creates is also called on to restore creation and this divine action serves but one original design. If not, then God is made overly dependent on the human initiative of sin, and a chasm opens between creator and redeemer. In the restoration that God effects through Jesus, however, something new is offered. The traditional distinction between *natural* and *supernatural* was, in fact, forged to identify exactly what is *new* in the "new creation," namely a transformation of human potential for friendship with God. And when friendship with the creator of all is possible, an entirely new relation of human beings with the rest of creation is possible as well.[13] This natural/supernatural distinction, however, has been used to separate humankind and the natural world and to set them at odds. The distinction has even served to absolve the church of any concern for the natural world.

The way to undo such misuses of the distinction cannot lie in overlooking (or even denying) the reality it was meant to mark. Rather, we need to exploit its original intent for the purpose of rightly relating creation and redemption. Rather than propose a "new story" of emergence that obscures the precise import of the *supernatural,* we need to learn how to see the new creation as restoring God's original intent precisely by transforming what we have come to know of human potentiality and humankind's relation to the rest of nature, and hence to our creator and to other human beings.

3

WHY "THE CHRIST MUST SUFFER
AND SO ENTER INTO HIS GLORY"

In our initial survey of Jesus' mission to restore the original
peace of God's creation, we touched on the question of why he had
to suffer, but it deserves much closer attention. It might be helpful
to begin by recalling an observation, attributed to G. K. Chesterton,
that "original sin is the only empirically verified Christian doctrine," and then to ask how the original order of creation could possibly be restored. There is no doubt that something is radically
wrong with the world, and surely much depends on the diagnosis
of that wrong. Christian teaching in this regard is rooted in Paul's
reading of Genesis 3. In the previous chapter we suggested that
what makes the man and the woman's sin originative is not the
transgression as such, but their subsequent attempt at cover-up.

What is the teaching the Christian church has derived from
Genesis 3, relying on Paul's reading of the text? At the outset we
must say that *sin* is used analogously when we speak of personal
sin and of original sin. Normally, when we use the word *sin* we
refer to an action of which a person is guilty, yet it cannot be
Adam's guilt that is mysteriously passed on to the entire human
race; guilt is nontransferable. It is rather the response of both the
man and the woman to their action that is presented as an archetypal story to explain the pervasive character of evil in the world

as we know it. Yet perhaps our culture needs to pause a moment before that statement.

Medievals used to ask such questions as whether there is more evil than good in the universe. Thomas Aquinas's answer involved an initial distinction, as was his wont, between the world of nature and that of culture. The natural order of things, he suggests, displays on balance more good than evil—despite natural calamities and disasters—when we marvel at the intricacies of generation, of DNA (for us) and the rest. Even Darwin's random selection can function only against a background of incredible order, which alone allows such infinitesimal random mutations to have the effects they can have. When we look at the human world, however, Aquinas allowed that "evil, for the most part, prevails."[1] The matter-of-factness with which he puts it makes one wonder whether the culture-critics are right when they say that we children of the Enlightenment lost faith in human progress after the First World War. Do we not spontaneously hope that alterations in repressive political arrangements, for example, will issue in something better? How else explain the euphoria-cum-disillusion that followed after the collapse of the Berlin wall and the demise of the Soviet Union. Could we anticipate the deadly spate of internecine warfare, of "ethnic cleansing," or of tribal animosities fueling mutual annihilation? Not many believed rhetoric of a "new world order," to be sure, for the context of its utterance—the Persian Gulf conflict—hardly inspired visions of anything new, yet does not "hope spring eternal" in many of us? As we shall see, it is precisely the Christian diagnosis (of original sin) that will allow us to distinguish *hope* from *optimism*—a devilishly difficult thing to do, as it turns out.[2] Once we realize how deeply we are mired in the context of *sin,* we should better understand Aquinas's apparent insouciance in observing that evil, for the most part, prevails in human affairs.

The analytic diagnosis of the human condition runs as follows. The clumsy and obvious attempt at cover-up in Genesis 3, with the man abdicating responsibility and laying it on the woman while the woman does the same in regard to the serpent, has all the earmarks of a children's story: Very serious things are being presented in cartoon-like fashion. What is so serious, of course, is the "self-deception," which Herbert Fingarette helped us to identify. On his analysis, as we have seen, this capacity to deceive ourselves allows us to eschew responsibility for wrongdoing by calling what we are engaged in by some other name. In the story it is the serpent who promotes this strategy, convincing Eve that the action will not be wrongdoing so much as the key to a new understanding of things, and Adam telling himself that he should please his spouse. Moreover, once we play the game with ourselves about our actual intentions, we are pleased to have the charade confirmed by the society of which we are a part. And the more set our actual masks become, the more we settle into a masquerade. Is this not the picture we see around us? Despite individual good intentions, there is pervasive political corruption and maldistribution of needed resources. There is no hint here of transmission of guilt, but simply a context in which it becomes increasingly difficult for an individual to do the right thing, thanks to a pervasive environment where conformity leads to success. Something radical is required to alter this context—something akin to "redemption."

Since it is difficult to put aside preconceived notions concerning original sin, a comparison of Genesis 3 with the Qur'anic teaching may diffuse some long-standing polemics. We have seen already how a Muslim analysis of the human condition turns on *jâhiliyya:* a state of ignorance and error. This is so pervasive that a divine revelation is required for human beings to find a "straight path." Those who languish in ignorance and error, moreover, usually fail to realize that fact until they are confronted with some sort of revelation. And then it will be "something divine" that allows them to respond to the revelation, and that can be traced back to the original gift of creation: human reason.

What makes the revelation of the Qur'an authentic is its offer of a "straight path" out of an impossible situation—impossible, that is, for human beings to rectify on their own. So the long-standing contention that "original sin" has no place in Islam because God forgave Adam forthwith (e.g., Qur'an 20:122) is quite beside the point. The point is a diagnosis of the current situation locating the source of evil in pervasive human arrangements rather than in God's original intent. What the Christian and Muslim traditions have in common is a negative assessment of our condition without divine assistance. The human situation cannot simply be repaired. Despite the recent and misguided apologetic of Islam as a "rational religion" (whatever that might be), Christians and Muslims alike acknowledge the need for "divine grace." Where they differ, of course, is in identifying its source. Just how significant that difference will turn out to be has already been suggested; it involves understanding why "the Christ must suffer and so enter into his glory."

René Girard's analysis of the roots of violence will help us understand the Christian diagnosis and remedy for our situation.[3] He begins with a bow to Plato's candid admission that implementing his elaborate scheme in the *Republic* would involve persuading everyone of the truth of the "noble lie" regarding their inherent place in society. Girard goes on to formulate an illuminating thesis: To the extent that a human society is founded on a lie, just to that extent its leaders will be constrained to resort to violence to keep the lie intact. Lies have a way of coming to light, especially as the young may ask embarrassing questions about standing arrangements. Moreover, if the lie is central to the foundations of the polity, eradicating it will threaten the very existence of the state, which its leaders cannot afford. The truth of this thesis can be variously illustrated, but it is poignantly exhibited in the outright antithesis between two founding documents of the United States of America: a Declaration of Independence that proposes that "all men are created equal" with a Constitution asserting the lie (conveniently called a "compromise") that "slaves are to be treated as three-fifths of a person." That contradiction would before long foment the bloody "war between the states," abetted, of course, by cultural and economic interests. In another time and place Gandhi would remind us of the truth of Girard's thesis by his lifelong insistence that the means employed to gain independence will inescapably characterize the polity that emerges. That same truth dogged politics in the state of Israel until recently, where the past records of successive heads of state gave a hollow ring to their denunciation of Palestinian violence.

Girard's thesis adds something to the Genesis archetypal rendering of a pervasive human state of deception: the stake that state power inevitably has in maintaining the status quo. Girard highlights the specific need for those in power to maintain themselves and their polity. In a study so entitled, he shows how this entire drama can easily be made to turn on a *scapegoat*—someone whose death can apparently satisfy the need for "purification" while avoiding the herculean task of admitting guilt and seeking real reform. This analysis has the advantage of strengthening more traditional psychological ones like those of Augustine. Girard provides a staunchly political perspective, adding a note of realism to the drama of the crucifixion of Jesus. Yet since Augustine has received a quite consistently bad press of late, a word about him will not be remiss.

Our analysis of Genesis 3 roots sin in the climate of self-deception, a common human ploy that both facilitates our wrongdoing and provides a stake in conforming to the resultant status quo. In his *Confessions* Augustine offers a similar understanding of his own proper sin of ambition—the more immediate block to his accepting the light of divine grace, despite the man's continuing complaints about sensuality.[4] His analysis of a youthful escapade of stealing and trashing a neighbor's pears with his friends is even more probing. Augustine lays bare the self-destructive character of sin better than the Genesis story can or need do. On his retrospective reading of this episode, what is wrong about the action is its complete senselessness, something the self-deceiving dynamics of sin effectively masks (2, vi). (The Medievals explore this dimension in the celebrated "sin of the angels," wherein individuals undistracted by passion of any sort, and so clearly understanding their proper good, nonetheless rejected it.) It is one more mark of Augustine's acute psychological insight that he can use a childhood prank to illustrate the utterly self-defeating nature of sin. It may also be one more sign of the obtuseness of some current readers who bring forth the pear tree incident as one more instance of Augustine's being "hung up" on sin!

Analyses like those of Augustine and Girard point us in the direction of grasping why Jesus "had to suffer and so enter into his glory." There are at least two senses of "had to" in this pregnant line from Luke. Jesus had to undergo suffering because it was inevitable, given the human context we have sketched. But he also had to suffer in order to open us to the truth of how we continue to sustain that very context. And that is what Chesteron's quip misses: Just as those suffering from ignorance and error tended to remain ignorant of that fact until confronted with the Qur'an, so the observation that there is "something wrong" can remain idle until confronted with a full-scale diagnosis like the one revelation offers. Indeed, the "myth of human perfectibility" may well represent a lived corollary of a secular mentality, and so be a quite natural offspring of the Enlightenment. It is a delicious irony to propose that myths might spring from a thoroughgoing commitment to pure reason, yet it also suggests why it proves so difficult for those without the benefit of an analysis inspired by the gracious action of God to distinguish *hope* from *optimism.* For we must have some hope to motivate any initiative, especially the more clearly we are regarding the true shape of the situation in which we anticipate acting, yet a candid assessment of the human situation makes it quite difficult to suspect that "I could do any better." But if I am to act at all, I must pretend that

that is the case, and the result is what we call optimism, or unfounded hope!

Jesus did not engage in unfounded hope for making things better, since "he knew what was in human beings" (Jn 2:25). Indeed, the very scope of his mission to restore the original order of God's creation is what made it necessary that he suffer. For the self-deceived and self-destructive initiative of human beings that is sin had disturbed God's order, and sin is resistant to straightforward repair. Indeed, Jesus knew that. And the inevitable suffering that he would undergo (since the world of his time was governed by powers not unlike those of any other time of human history) constituted the very action that would open those willing to face it to understand their true situation. The entire drama of the cross is theandric—that is, a joint divine-human production, so to accept the diagnosis of sin as its cause *is* to receive the cure. Admission of our culpability opens us to the divine forgiveness freely offered by the One who freely bestows our existence. That is the meaning of Jesus' resurrection and of our participation in it. The two are, indeed, one action; the head of the body now lives, having died that the body might live. The manner of Jesus' death is crucial, since his suffering attests to the fact that God's creation could not be restored directly, even by the One through whom it has its very being. And his resurrection attests that the restoration and transformation of creation will be entrusted to sinners who have tasted the Lord's forgiveness and can give witness to that fact "from Jerusalem to the ends of the earth" (Lk 24:47; Acts 1:8).

The context in which that charge is given (Lk 24:36–49) tells it all. The resurrected Jesus suddenly appears in the midst of those who had left him to his ignominious fate a few days before. He queries: "Why are you troubled, and why do questionings arise in your hearts?" Why, indeed? Self-recrimination even more than doubt would have afflicted them. Jesus' asking for something to eat underscores Luke's apologetic intent here; he is truly risen, body and spirit. But the dramatic context is yet more compelling.

It must have dawned on each of the disciples in a flash: He has returned here—to us! That action of returning to them would say more than words: Whatever you have done or not done, however you may have deserted me by your action or inaction, is forgiven! And it is that very forgiveness that the disciples would witness to the ends of the earth. They experienced it in the recesses of their hearts—those hearts that had now been opened to see clearly how they had colluded in the destructive actions executed by the powers that be. No realization could be at once more devastating or more liberating, thanks to the power of God. The forgiveness of Jesus, extended by the risen Lord, truly effects a new creation.

4

HUMAN DEATH, HUMAN SUFFERING

In his provocative article that helped to shape this inquiry, John McDade reminds us that "the very witness of martyrdom is an assertion that there is, in all seriousness, a more destructive reality than death, namely, the possibility of rejecting God's love."[1] He criticizes approaches like Moltmann's and Jungel's, which focus on God's death in Jesus, presuming that "death is the point of vulnerability within creation." For McDade, however, "death is a biological fact of all organic life." He acknowledges that "at the level of our metaphors, death and sin interact, and death stands as the symbol of sinful destructiveness; [but] at the level of actuality, they are separable and ought to be distinguished." Thus when Paul says that "the wages of sin is death" (Rom 6:23), we need not interpret the biological fact of death as the consequence of sin. Rather, because of the way in which sin has become the context of our lives, death has been turned into the reality we most feel and fear. In a disordered creation, death comes to stand for something yet more sinister than itself. Given a world marked by self-deception, the fact of death now serves as a metaphor for the self-destructiveness of sin, which is the root of disorder in creation.

But what, then, of the promise of eternal life? If death itself is not actually the consequence of sin but becomes its expression, is "eternal life" only a metaphor for escaping the human condition? Indeed, that is the burden of some relatively recent writing that would reconcile us with our mortality.[2] These efforts to interpret the resurrection as something other than a pledge of eternal life, however, are really intent on neutralizing the reward structure of heaven/hell as unworthy of authentic faith. And that is a recurring theme in Islam as well as among Christian saints.[3] Indeed we should recall how the gospels, notably John, speak about "eternal life." It has nothing to do with rewards, an "after-life," or the indefinite prolongation of this one. Eternal life refers to the new kind of life that the followers of Jesus are already living—a life that cannot end because it is a participation in God's own life—and "to God everyone is alive"(Lk 20:38). So the New Testament itself offers a picture of new life in Christ that is far from palliative, and the outlines of that picture become clearer to believers as their faith matures.

By a "palliative picture" we mean something offered to a person to offset the human fear of death. That fear has been dramatized in an archetypal manner in the myth of Gilgamesh.[4] Yet this story contains its own critique of a naive wish to live forever. Utnapishtim, who does go on living forever, is depicted living a very dreary life. The myth seems to suggest that the impending certainty of death, fearful as it may be, focuses the human spirit on the meaning and joys of this life. Utnapishtim enjoys no such focus. Gilgamesh, despite his suffering in the face of death, learns the value of life. For all that, however, nothing completely eradicates our ubiquitous fear of death.

Paul may, in fact, be exploiting this fear by linking sin with death. Indeed, the pagans to whom he was commissioned to carry the good news would have been quite incapable of responding to a Jesus preached to his own people as "Messiah" or "Christ," so Paul must focus on the evil they *feel*—death, using it as a metaphor for something yet more sinister: "The law of the Spirit of life in Christ Jesus has set me free from the law of sin and death" (Rom 8:2). Alienation from our own selves as creatures of God will be evidenced in our horror of death. Human beings, called to acknowledge the gift of creation by responding to Jesus' mission of re-creation, can refuse to do so and continue to cling to the disordered self that shares complicity for a disordered world. Rather than recognize life as a gift that is given and asked to be returned, we fiercely clutch as our own the life we have made for ourselves, quite unable to let that life go.

Ernest Becker's *Denial of Death* supports such a reading. He notes how a simple fear of death easily escalates into terror when death looms as the destroyer of my self-project.[5] In the measure that I see my task in life as forging the self that I must make, then death becomes the great destroyer. And the self seems to become a self-project as soon as one ceases to ask about its origins, for then a presumption emerges quite spontaneously: I must have brought myself about, preoccupied as I am with shaping the self at hand. The burden of Becker's work is to show how this syndrome dissolves once we accept the universe as freely created. Then my life, mortal as it is, becomes a gift bestowed, which invites me to *spend* it so that it is returned enhanced to its giver. The fear of death will not evaporate, but the dynamics that escalate it into terror are displaced and neutralized by the visage of a creator.

Suffering can be transformed as well. For understanding creation as a gift has the effect of releasing me from the onus of a solitary life-project. Once unburdened, what appeared as obstacles may even become opportunities. Illness, for example, may be welcomed as a time to learn how to receive from others; financial failure may be the occasion for reassessing all my values. Suffering will invariably involve pain of some sort, but need not be—nor even feel—destructive, so long as life is not viewed only as my life-project! Becker forcibly reminds us that the language of "life-project" seems inescapable, however, especially for Westerners.[6] Indeed, it is as inexorable as our desire to be first, so Jesus' way of addressing that need can teach us something about dealing with our penchant for making our lives into projects. Jesus suggested a paradoxical way of becoming first: to make oneself last! He did not tell us *not* to want to be first; knowing us as he did, Jesus knew that would be fruitless (Jn 2:25). But he did offer us a *way* that could utilize our very impulse to subvert it—a kind of spiritual *jujitsu.* Become first by seeking to be last!

Will a ploy like that work with life-projects? Yes, if we accept the other part of Jesus' advice regarding our desire to be first: Set out to become the servant of all. What constitutes the inherently solitary life-project immortalized by Nietzsche is the refusal to serve anyone—at least anyone else! Therein lies the rub; for if we are serving no one else, then we are serving ourselves. And as Socrates reminded us long ago, what part of ourselves are we serving in serving ourselves? I am reminded of a friend who happened to remark to a colleague that he couldn't really be bothered about some of the shenanigans of academe, because he served the church. When they met a few days later, the colleague admitted that he had been thinking about that remark and had concluded that he served himself. To which my friend—an astute ethicist— retorted: "Too bad; I hope that doesn't mean you *have* to do everything you *want* to do!" That quip reminds us how we are creatures of multiple wants, and we can never be sure which of our desires we will be serving in trying to serve ourselves. Autonomy turns out not to be so autonomous after all. It seems we are in need of an external point of reference whereby we can be assured of whom we really serve and what we truly want.

But can we ever trust an external point of reference? Here is where the pattern of revelation embodied in the Qur'an and its "coming down" to Muhammed may be helpful. The recurring rhetorical dynamic of the Qur'an has ostensibly self-sufficient human beings confronted by a commanding word from God. This word reminds us that we are not sufficient unto ourselves; we are creatures. The command from God announces that our creator is offering us a way—a "straight path"—by which we can live so as to return the gift of ourselves to its giver. It also tells us how to express gratitude for the gift of all that we are and of all-that-is, as well as for this word from God informing us of mind-bending and life-shaping *facts* of which we would otherwise be ignorant. So while the Qur'an may come to us from outside ourselves in the preaching of Muhammad and later of the Muslim community *[umma]*, our response to it wells up from within. Our created nature *[fitra]* can recognize the voice of the creator when it speaks. So in the end, what the Qur'an offers is not something *external* to us; as the voice of our creator, it rather addresses us from within. The creator's guidance leads us out of ourselves, paradoxically, into our true selves. The better term for such a reference point, therefore, is not "external" but "transcendent." The One who transcends us as our creator is also "closer to [us] than [our] jugular vein" (Qur'an 5:16).

A similar dynamic can be observed in John's gospel where Jesus likens himself to the good shepherd, noting that "I know my own and my own know me, as the Father knows me and I know the Father" (10:14–15). The image of a shepherd is particularly telling, since sheep are notoriously stupid. This unflattering image of ourselves can suggest that a kind of homing instinct— dumb yet sure—guides our response to the presence of the Word-made-flesh. If Jesus is the One through whom all-that-is comes to be, then our response to him will not be to someone alien. Here again, that response is to our most authentic self, and serving Jesus will bring us freedom, or even better, restore our original freedom. The Qur'an, however, more explicitly connects revealer with creator. Once that is done, then the voice of revelation may come to us from outside ourselves but nonetheless correspond to what is deepest within us because our very existence consists in being related to this One.

Understanding the Muslim and Christian scriptures in this way can transform the way we look at our lives. We will continue to think of them and to describe them as *projects,* no doubt, yet now animated and directed by the need to return them with gratitude to their original source. Seeing the One who reveals as that source can also teach us a fresh use of the term *transcendent,* one that evokes immanence as well.[7] Thomas Aquinas connects the good shepherd parable with the Qur'an for us by reminding us of another connection: "The proper effect of the first and most universal cause, God, is the *to-be* of things" (ST 1.45.5), and this "*to-be* is innermost in each thing" (1.8.1). So it will be utterly natural for us to respond, as sheep to shepherd, to the One who "says 'Be' and it is" (Qur'an 2:117). What better way to recall the inner connection between the first two articles of the creed!

Let us return to suffering and death. How does this picture of revealer-creator alter things from within? To begin with, much that presents itself as suffering on a solitary life-project agenda dissolves in a more cosmic horizon. Think of the Buddhist remedy for suffering: Eliminate desire and suffering will disappear. Jesus' way of subverting our desire to be first comes close to it in practice. To the extent that suffering means that my projects are blocked, then letting go of them as *mine* attenuates the suffering and eventually reduces it to nothing. Is that not what the Buddhist strategy comes to? With Jesus, the Buddha's wisdom also realizes that *desire* itself cannot be eliminated. But I can distance myself from the imperiousness of a particular desire by refusing to own it—by "disappropriating" it as no longer my own. What if, however, this project of mine is intended to be in the service of something that is not mine at all, something larger like justice? Then may I simply let go of it? Hardly, both Buddha and Jesus would answer. I can still, however, let go of it as my own.[8]

What good will that do? It will remind me how *inconsistent* it is to insist that a particular project be in the service of a larger ideal and yet continue to claim it as my own—inconsistent in the pragmatic sense of *consistency,* in which my life must line up with my assertions. This is a sense of consistency that will allow us to understand why Gandhi insisted on "renouncing the fruits of one's action." He grasped that the very best we can do is to do everything possible toward promoting an ideal, and then leave its realization to forces beyond our control. For any further attempt to manipulate those forces and so assure that *my* action is efficacious will invariably do violence to the dynamics of the action itself by introducing an untoward element of *me* into the mix. Much that we call "suffering" can be written off as the effect of our holding on to the inauthentic self, which Jesus told us to let go if we would truly live. This is not easily "written off," certainly, yet written off nonetheless. Buddha and Jesus effectively concur.

Note that this is not a strategy for "making sense" of suffering so much as it is one of distinguishing ersatz suffering, better called frustration, from real suffering. Such a strategy leads us to focus on the latter. Before leaving frustrations behind, however, recall how frustrated ambitions can be a powerful incentive to get me out of my own self and into a wider world. In fact, we seem to learn best from our failures, once we can bring ourselves to recognize them. We seem to learn in a privileged space carved out between our ambitions and our true self.

The arresting biblical story of the "binding of Isaac" helps to make this point and gives us a view of real suffering and the way to meet it. Remember that the promises the Lord had made to Abraham all were made in terms of making *him* a great nation through his offspring. So the very form in which God's promise had been made—a form the sheik Abraham could comprehend—left room within it for him to exalt himself. But he was commanded to do the unthinkable, to *sacrifice* the only son of his old age and the very means of Abraham's being made into a great nation. To obey that stark command would be for him to put God's will before his own ambitions. (It would upset everything else as well, as Kierkegaard and others have remarked: the very integrity of a God who commands such a thing.) God's integrity may have been saved by not demanding what had been commanded, but in the process Abraham's ambition certainly was effectively severed from the promise. Indeed, Abraham's son had been taken away from him; Isaac was no longer his possession but the instrument of God's promise. Yet without that horrible trial and indubitable suffering, Abraham would never have known whether he was responding to God for God's sake or for his own: to become a great nation!

By invoking the relation of parents to child, this story carries us beyond ambition with its attendant frustrations to the most elemental and binding sort of love, and to the genuine suffering such love engenders. Surely there is no clearer example of suffering among humans than that of parents' having to watch their child suffer, or to "lose a child," as the English idiom puts it. Even here, as Abraham's severe and direct testing exhibits, there is a space that the suffering parents need to carve between the child and themselves. It is hardly for anyone else to say that, of course, but it is crucial that we see it, for such an insight can lead us further into Jesus' suffering and into suffering itself. When we think of what such parents go through, or refugees and victims of ethnic violence, we cannot understand how such people go on. Yet we know they do. Often a kind of shock or numbing allows people to carry on almost automatically. But it seems possible to go on positively only when we can move beyond needing to repair the hurt done to *us*.

Here one's response will differ greatly if the loss results from violence or from accidental or natural causes. In cases involving violence, we must be moved to a compassion capable of embracing the culprits along with the victims, whom we love. In short, our capacity for loving has to be expanded well beyond those we naturally love to include even our enemies. As we know well enough, we cannot do that ourselves; we must be moved to it. Gandhi suggested we could be so moved by the very "force of truth" *[satyagraha]*. For Christians, that truth-force will be focused in Jesus' suffering.

Perhaps Jesus' suffering offers the only pure case there is, for he had no ambitions to be frustrated. Jesus sought only the "will of the Father," by which he meant that very order of creation to be

restored. Aquinas avers that since in his very person Jesus is the
"divine wisdom which constitutes this order" (ST 1.47.1), he
cannot but be intent on restoring it. So Jesus must suffer because
over the generations we humans have succeeded in obscuring the
order of creation. But if Jesus is intent on restoring creation, then
he did have an ambition. He wanted to restore those traces of
God's hand in creation so that human beings could live in peace.
If, indeed, that was the Father's will, was it not also Jesus' ambition—his desire? Certainly. But as we have seen, Jesus was wise
enough to know that nothing he could *do* would be able to restore
the order of creation; what had destroyed it was sin, that peculiar
inversion of action of which human beings are capable. And
nothing could simply turn that around.

Jesus' suffering then consists in his realization that nothing he
could do would restore God's original peace. Quite independent
of any personal ambition, he was called by the truth itself to a
mission incapable of fulfillment in any ordinary sense of doing
something to carry it out. There was nothing else to do but suffer,
just as there was nothing else the organized disorder we call "the
world" could do but try to eliminate him. Finally, in the face of
personal and social sin, in the midst of the collective disorder
obscuring God's original order of creation, nothing but Jesus'
suffering could move us to do what each of us needs to do:
acknowledge ourselves as sinners and ask forgiveness. Hence the
sheer economy, as the early church writers loved to call it, of
Jesus' mission and the suffering attending it.

The lesson for Christians begins with distinguishing genuine
suffering from the frustrations attending ambition. These latter we
can come to recognize as heaven-sent. Such frustrations provide
ways of detaching us from frivolous or even destructive aims and
goals. They can assist isolated spectators to enter into the human
condition. Real suffering, however, cannot be heaven-sent, even
though it is divinely permitted. And the more we accept it, the
more we will enter into the suffering of Jesus. No one can ask for

this, since we cannot want evil. Nonetheless, real suffering offers a unique way of discovering the mystery of God revealed in a "Christ who must suffer before entering into his glory." Thus suffering offers a privileged entry into that divine glory.

Despite our penchant to couple them, suffering and death are quite distinct realities. As we have unveiled it here, genuine suffering testifies to the presence of evil—either of malice or of a searing privation, as in the "loss" of a loved one. But death comes naturally; we are all "terminal cases." Yet we are able to accept what comes naturally, the ending of our life, only in the measure that we have been moved to see our lives as something other than a life-project. If the focus has been shifted to returning a gift, then we can consider the impending end as offering a completed gift, however imperfect, to the One who gifted us with life initially and has always sustained us. Doubtless, suffering of different sorts will have had a hand in detaching us from the propensity to consider our lives as our projects. Given that fact, suffering and death deserve to be coupled. There must be a radical kind of detachment inherently associated with knowing that our end is imminent, and detachment is ever painful. Death has often been called the final detachment, when we have to let go even of the gift itself, "renouncing the fruits of our actions" and entrusting ourselves to the mercy of God, the creator-redeemer.

Both Christian and Muslim consciousness has been schooled to link sin and death by means of the impending judgment. The Qur'an never ceases to connect death with judgment, and in both Qur'an and New Testament the judgment is not merely individual. It is preeminently social, indeed cosmic: the "end of the world." The Qur'an provides a useful clue in linking origins with ending as well, for it reminds us how easy it is for the God who creates from nothing to restore the dead to life. " 'Who will revive these bones when they have rotted away?' Say: He will revive them Who produced them at the first, for He is the knower of every creation....His command, when He intends a thing, is only that He says to it: Be! and it is" (36:79, 82). If the accent in the Qur'an is especially on human beings, that is a function of its role as a "warning." In the New Testament, however, the emphasis is on aligning the judgment with the end of the universe as we know it; the whole of creation is transformed for Christians into a "new heaven and a new earth...the holy city, new Jerusalem" (Rv 21:1–2).

So while death for us is a biological fact, it is, to be sure, also much more. Human destiny is offered as a microcosm for that of the universe, which has been given its destiny in God's free initiation of creating it, as revelation informs us. If our lives are given a point by the impending judgment, so the universe is given a point in the announcement that it too will end. The universe need not have had a beginning, nor need it have an end. Both creation and judgment come to human beings as a revelation, that is, a way of being freely invited into God's confidence regarding the original divine order. We are told how it was and how it will be. This is not "information," but an invitation to take up responsibility for our own lives. The Qur'an represents our taking up such a responsibility as the fulfillment of God's original covenant with Adam (33:72). The "trust" that we humans failed to carry out can be thus restored.

It sharpens this picture to regard the trust originally offered to us in the light of Jesus' mission to restore the original order of creation. This would allow us to see the judgment as focused on how we have lived our lives in relation to one another *and* to the rest of God's creation. Heretofore this dimension has been missing in Christianity, but it seems a natural development to elaborate it now. As we have recently awakened to a new species of sin—social sin—why not let our eyes be opened to our collusion with ecological disasters? Often enough social sin and ecological sin are already partners in crime. We are, it seems, only at the beginning of a journey to discover the full implications of Christ's mission to restore the original order of creation. Coming to understand suffering and death in the perspective that has been suggested should spur us on to accept responsibility for the universe as well as for our own lives. At least this perspective allows us to see the classical Christian story of beginnings and endings as a unity.

5

THE ECONOMY OF THE SACRAMENTS

It is tempting for theologians to give a nod to newfound ecological awareness by adding to treatments of the sacraments a chapter that links them with creation. Such attempts, however well intended, cannot bridge the gap carved between the first two articles of the creed; the people who write such books have been shaped by an agenda in which anthropological concerns dominate. In fact, since Vatican II, creative inquiry into the sacraments has proposed a rich vision of human development correlated with the rites of initiation, continuing nourishment in the eucharist, vocational commitment, reconciliation, and illness.[1] Stimulated by an official reform of the rites, this writing distinguishes itself from earlier preoccupation with an "ontology" of the sacraments—*what* is happening and *how* it is being effected. The newer approach, rather, uses ritual patterns as a prism for displaying the human dimensions of sacramental action. By focusing on *sign,* questions of "causality" are transposed into a properly *sacramental* key accenting anthropological realities. In this way the sacraments can be appreciated as human activities carried out in a believing community, with the goal of enhancing its unity by relating that community to the Lord and its members to one another.[2] But valuable as this is, now we clearly need to find a way to move beyond the anthropological to incorporate all of creation.

Does not the customary emphasis on materials used in the rituals like water and oil, bread and wine, already make us conscious of the earth? That time-honored approach surely helps to connect us with creation, but has not led to participating in its restoration. Is there a way that would? Is there a theological approach to the sacraments that includes their implications for the whole of creation and not only for human beings? Yes: focusing on Jesus' mission to restore God's original peace. Just as we discovered fresh insights into the suffering of Jesus and of human beings in that perspective, so might we see new connections between the sacraments and creation. Our approach will be to look at individual sacraments, or at least groupings of them, to see how a focus on the mission of Jesus could affect our understanding of the whole sacramental economy, and how that in turn can alter our understanding of creation.

BAPTISM AND CONFIRMATION, AND EUCHARIST

Baptism and confirmation, as sacraments of Christian initiation, bestow on believers a priestly character, commissioning them to an active role in "restoring all things in Christ"(Eph 1:10). If this teaching has been accepted in anthropological terms—as indeed it has—we can easily extend the reach of that commission (as Paul himself does) to include the entire universe of creation. The logic of the matter is simple: Since these sacraments initiate persons into participation in the community of the faithful "with all its rights and duties" (Baptismal Rite), then their manner of perceiving that commission will directly correlate with the church's self-understanding of its mission. Vatican II disseminated a fresh theological view of the church as church-to-the-world, notably through the pastoral constitution "Church in the Modern World *[Gaudium et Spes]*." The call today is to appreciate how the church's mission reaches beyond the inherently human world envisioned in these conciliar documents to

embrace the entire created universe. Within that horizon, followers of Jesus will come to see baptism and confirmation as commissioning them to respond to his call from the Father to restore
everything in creation to its original blessing. For that to happen,
however, the church itself must continue to grow in realizing the
multiple ways of sharing in Jesus' mission. Only then can the
sacraments themselves embody such an understanding, and
Christians grasp the implications for their lives. Baptism and
confirmation will then properly initiate believers into the "new
creation" in all its dimensions.

Broadly speaking, the eucharist is linked with baptism and confirmation because it initiates into *full* participation in the Christian
community. But unlike these one-time rites, the eucharist continues regularly to sustain the life and mission of believers. In its
shape as a meal and with its goal of providing nourishment for
mind and heart, the eucharist is especially open to incorporating
ever-widening horizons of human aspiration and endeavor.[3] The
offertory prayers, adapted from the Jewish liturgy, pointedly
express the relation of this sacramental meal to creation:

> Blessed are you, Lord, God of all creation. Through your good-
> ness we have this bread to offer, which earth has given and human
> hands have made. It will become for us the bread of life.

> Blessed are you, Lord, God of all creation. Through your good-
> ness we have this wine to offer, fruit of the vine and work of
> human hands. It will become our spiritual drink.

These short prayers stem immediately from the liturgical
renewal that preceded and continued the ecclesial renewal of Vatican II. It is significant that they signal the origins of the church's
eucharistic celebration in the Jewish blessing-tradition of *beraka,*
as well as presage a theology uniting creation with redemption.
That theology would put matters like this: In the eucharistic celebration what is transformed is the entire universe *as* human

beings are part of it and relate themselves to it. Jesus' suffering, death, and resurrection—which the eucharist embodies—effected a transformation in principle of the way human beings relate to the world, thus potentially transforming everything in creation. So it is natural for believers to look at the consecrated bread and wine and "see the world," as a friend once said to me. Indeed, if the universe is restored to its original order in principle, then participating in the eucharist is the way in which believers learn to take part in that restoration.

RECONCILIATION, ANOINTING OF SICK, HOLY ORDERS, AND MATRIMONY

What about the other sacraments? How would focusing on the mission of Jesus to restore creation's original peace affect our understanding of reconciliation, sacrament of the sick, orders, and matrimony? First and foremost, by showing how these sacraments combine to structure the *mission of the community* into which believers are initiated and sustained by baptism, confirmation, and the eucharist. Much has been written about the role they play in meeting moments of critical significance in our personal journeys. What our refiguration will show is the way in which they prepare us as members of this community to relate properly to the gift of creation.

Reconciliation reminds us of the character and will of the God we worship, since the sins we confess, formally defined as "offenses against God," reveal our conception of and relation to the God we worship. In fact, it might be argued that no sacrament has undergone a more radical renewal since Vatican II than that of reconciliation, both in its form and its content. And both were envisaged in the liturgical reforms, since it was clear that what we confess is closely linked with the way we go about confessing it. What could not have been foreseen by these reforms, however, was the way in which the very notion of *sin* was transformed at the same time by the enveloping culture. An influential book written by Karl Menninger, a psychiatrist, in the 1970s and entitled *Whatever Became of Sin?* sums it up nicely.[4] A "therapeutic culture" had preempted the language of "sin," replacing it with that of "illness." One no longer sought absolution but counsel; guilt had been superseded by "guilt feelings," and these could be explained away without recourse to forgiveness.

That culture, however, no longer reigns supreme. While it is far from dead, its limitations have become far more evident. Indeed, one may expect a sequel to Menninger, entitled *It Came Back as Addiction!* The current flourishing of "twelve-step" programs, largely under the aegis of churches, testifies to the way in which addiction has become the current idiom for sin. Some may criticize these programs for having allowed themselves to be captured by a therapeutic culture in adopting a "disease model" for addiction, yet the strong Augustinian fabric of the twelve-step programs themselves suggests that "disease" is being employed to forestall others' judgment rather than to eliminate or even minimize the addict's responsibility. Augustine dominates the first step, where addicts acknowledge they are powerless in the face of their particular "poison," and have given themselves over to "a higher power" in order to be empowered to take the further steps they need to take. The arresting paradox—that only by first admitting our powerlessness can we be empowered to act—is the upshot of Augustine's powerful personal experience related in his *Confessions.* So the dynamics of twelve-step programs conveys a strong sense of one's bondage and need for release and reconciliation, despite the strategic use of the language of illness— designed, I have suggested, to forestall adverse moral judgment rather than to abdicate responsibility. So admission of sin and the need for forgiveness return in a new key.

Anointing of the sick is certainly the sacrament whose administration has been most affected by the liturgical reforms. Changing the name from "extreme unction" says it all: What had been seen as a death-bed final farewell is now presented as part of a healing process. Experience confirms that this sacrament can help people explore the many dimensions of illness and healing, which become increasingly relevant as we are made aware of the limits as well as the wonders of modern medicine. This sacrament can be a powerful incentive to explore effectively and affectively, in a manner proper to each person, one's own relationship to human art in the larger scenario of nature. Here we are speaking largely of *attitudes*—characteristic ways human beings have of relating to their world—about which it is difficult for most of us to be articulate. But it is precisely such attitudes that virtually govern the healing process, notably our expectations of what the institution of medicine, and its practitioners, may be able to do for us.

Indeed, there is abundant evidence that one's attitude toward one's illness may be the single most important factor in healing, even in complete recovery.[5] (A friend with cancer was reading everything on the subject she possibly could—from technical scientific studies through literature about alternative medicine, to pamphlets on the latest pop therapies. When asked if these various approaches to dealing with cancer had anything in common, she remarked this: "Yes, only one thing. They all say that nothing counts more than the sufferer's attitude toward it.") So if the sacrament of the sick contributes to altering attitudes, that is no small contribution to the process of healing the person and, by extension, to healing the whole of a wounded creation. The need for sacramental action so conceived and executed is imperative in our culture, where technological innovations have called spontaneous attitudes into question and introduced profound ambivalence into many human hearts.

Is it appropriate to pray before we or our friends enter upon surgery, or is the effectiveness of that procedure simply a matter of the surgeon's skill? To be more nuanced: How do we pray? or what is it we pray for? or how do we feel about praying at such times? These questions signal some practical implications of the now-famous "secularization thesis," which holds that what people used to pray for they have now learned to entrust to the professional competence of, say, surgeons or airline pilots. But as many have noted, that is surely too crude an analysis of what happens. In Chapter 2 we mentioned the especially penetrating analysis regarding development experts who were baffled at the behavior of the Azande. Recall that when these people were presented with fertilizer, they simply combined that with their rituals rather than discarding the rituals. One commentator suggested a simple reason: The Azande had a richer view of human life and human art than the experts.[6] Indeed, the people understood that fertilizer helped increase their yield, but they also sensed that raising crops involved more than mere production. The work not only comprised their way of life, but linked them to the larger forces of the universe—patterns of precipitation or drought quite beyond the influence of fertilizers. In short, their traditional rituals reminded them that their work was more than work; it was their lifeline connecting them with a wider universe. And that connection demands celebration as well as entreaty.

So those who espouse the so-called secularization thesis may also be on the road to trivializing their lives, to turning themselves in their daily work into production machines, and forgetting that the most ordinary actions of our life are potentially rituals as well. Our daily work patterns are, in fact, patterns of relationship to many realities. To consider such relationships purely as *work* (itself regarded as *production*) easily brings us to employ ulterior means to escape from what has become an entrapment. As Ernest Becker remarks in concluding his *The Denial of Death:* "Modern man is drinking and drugging himself out of awareness, or he spends his time shopping, which is the same thing."[7] The parallel attitude with respect to illness is to entrust oneself to pharmaceutical or surgical means to "get well." Such a technological fix dispenses one from actually relating to one's illness; indeed, it dispenses from relating to oneself, and puts the onus for a cure on the physician or surgeon whose *patient* one then becomes. It is significant that physicians and surgeons themselves are increasingly wary of these attitudes on the part of their patients, finding them not really conducive to healing. Many medical doctors are beginning to lead people with whom they work to take an active part in their own cure. Active participation in their own healing requires people to understand and to undertake practices that will assist nature's processes.

The sacrament of the sick can elicit a "positive attitude" directed toward one's illness by engendering an acceptance that is quite at variance with resignation—more akin to Mary's "be it done unto me according to your will." For the sacramental ritual brings together scripture, prayer, oil and water, and the presence of caring friends along with a priest. These friends, with the ordained minister of the sacrament, remind persons who are incapacitated that they belong to a human community and to a church that takes an active interest in them. So the ritual invites those who are ill to utilize all the resources available to relate them to their illness, while placing it in the larger context of nature, culture, and grace. The very act of receiving the sacrament of the sick prods those subject to illness (or facing surgery) to remember that the technology that often surrounds them cannot be the last word, and that they remain capable of enunciating a further word of personal response.

This represents a form of empowerment by the Holy Spirit in the midst of physical and usually emotional diminishment that recalls persons to the resources of their faith community and to reserves present within themselves.[8] The sacramental ritual can often transform relations within the community as well, liberating people when necessary to speak of the unspeakable—death. Such a freedom enables friends to comfort those whom they otherwise would only attempt to "cheer up." In this way, the sacrament of the sick offers a paradigm for sacramental action more generally: to recall us to the community of faith in order to learn the proper attitude toward the activity in question, or to gain the right perspective on the dimension of human life at issue. This sacrament also happens best to illustrate our current thesis, for the attitude at stake in illness has to do with our relation to the rest of the natural world through our bodily connection with it.

Finally, to matrimony and holy orders, and the connections linking them from within. If the sacraments had no finality beyond constituting the community of faithful that we call church, then holy orders would take priority; it provides an inner structure for that body. But the sacraments also offer us ways to learn and to practice our participation in the mission of Jesus, so they are oriented well beyond church. To put it in other words, the sacraments show us how church is church-to-the-world. And if we take that to the next step and speak of church-to-the-universe, then matrimony easily holds the place of honor. Husband and wife are invited to fulfill the original pattern of creation for men and women, the pattern the biblical text says constitutes the image of God in humanity. Precisely in doing this, however, the couple shares intimately in the creative power of nature itself. Moreover, the family that normally results from matrimony is said to be the basic unit of society, so this sacrament scores high on an anthropological rating as well.

But plenty of restoration needs to be done in the case of matrimony, as cultural attitudes regarding the relative status of husband and wife in the relationship abundantly testify. As we have noted, it was in response to just such a cultural presumption regarding the marital relationship ("is it lawful for a *man* to put away his *wife*?") that Jesus articulated his mission as that of restoring creation to its original God-given order. We want to suggest that this restoration can be effected in terms of an ordering that is other than "hierarchical" in the ordinary sense of one being above and another below. Rather, the ordering that will ideally be exhibited between man and woman in marriage is identical to that which ought to be exhibited in a church structured by "holy orders." In order to carry this out, however, we shall have to restore confidence in two terms that have come upon hard times: *complementarity* and *hierarchy*. Indeed, we want to suggest that a proper understanding of *complementarity* offers a way of restoring the term *hierarchy* to its root meaning of "holy order," thus removing from this form of *order* any hint of what we normally associate with *hierarchy,* namely, an ordering of higher and lower. In the process, we may catch some glimpse of why the Hebrew scriptures regard the exemplary relationship of the human couple as offering the image of God in humankind.[9]

Let us begin by considering *complementarity*. To say that A complements B is to say that each has something the other lacks; it does not say what that something is. Because that something is not specified, *complements* is an analogous term, adapting its descriptive sense to each different context. Analogous terms are, of course, the bane of ideologues. For instance, those who are intent on offering a clear description of *how* men and women *generally* complement each other, along with those who rightly oppose such generalizations or fixed descriptions, conspire to neutralize a very rich expression and turn it into a polemical battleground. Rather, the notion of *complementarity* should lead us to understand a situation in which mutuality prevails and constitutes the inner dynamic of the relationship.

Apply this to matrimony—whose archetypal ordering Jesus invokes to articulate his mission as restoring God's original peace. In that original order men and women were to complement one another as they were created to do. Each would give to and use for the benefit of the other *whatever* were that person's unique gifts. Mutuality would nullify any license for "a man to put away his wife," first by challenging the ordering implicit in that phrase. Mutuality, moreover, would remind us that the bonding of marriage is forever because it reflects the *holy order* inherent in the universe as created through God's eternal word. In God's original order, then, the divine image—exemplified in the living exchange between a woman and a man—was intended to be fruitful on many levels: in generating offspring and in forming a community of the spouses. What the sacrament does is to bless the couple's intent to imitate in their lives God's original ordering. Yet the blessing must needs be far more than a simple confirmation, since the disorder human beings have wrought is probably more evident in this relationship between women and men than in any other. Once again, we discover the link between the redemptive activity of Jesus and the original order he set out to restore: by a suffering that alone could transform the systemic wrong in creation.

There is no formula for complementarity, but each marriage relationship that is fruitful knows its secret. Identifying *complementarity* with fixed roles trivializes the notion and evacuates its creative potential. As with all genuinely analogous terms, the only way to proceed is by way of examples. One cannot argue from preconceived patterns, since each relationship must discover its own form of complementarity in practice. Wedding anniversaries offer a particularly salient example, when partners will both insist that they would not be who and what they are without the other. In effect, each one gives credit to the other. (Similar relationships can be found in lifelong friendships and within vowed communities.) If we remain mesmerized by an ordering that must place one partner in a marriage above or below the other, then we need to invoke Paul's formula for forming a community of believers: "Let each one consider the other superior to themselves!" (Phil 2:3). That is Paul's version of Jesus' paradoxical advice for undermining our inborn desire to be first: "Whoever would be first, let that one be the servant of all and the last of all" (Mk 9:35). The Christian scriptures offer us a fresh meaning of *hierarchy* (or holy order) that specifically subverts the innate penchant we have for ranking, which we persist in dubbing "hierarchical."

One potent reason for that insidious identification surely lies in the notion of *hierarchy* that has flourished in the church, the

institution that speaks explicitly of "holy orders." It is commonplace that images of above and below dominate discourse relating those in orders to those who are not, yet it is equally obvious
how little such ways of speaking reflect what Jesus and Paul recommended, Moreover, since the discourse usually emanates
from those "in orders," it is easily suspected of being self-serv-
ing—or of serving power-relations.[10] In fact, whenever the accent
is on the *powers* reserved to those who are ordained, one can easily suspect the discourse of trying to legitimate power, and this
will happen notably when that power feels itself in jeopardy. But
what is the alternative? A quite simple one, really, and one that
emerges palpably in Vatican II's treatment of the church as the
"people of God," a priestly people ordered hierarchically.

Notice how easily the very mention of order in a Christian
community invokes an unreconstructed notion of *hierarchy,* with
some above and others below, and special powers reserved to
those placed above. Yet to speak of a priestly people is to remind
us all that the powers of the Spirit of Jesus are embodied in the
church itself, which then *ordains* certain ones to function in positions of leadership that are intended to *exemplify* the reality contained in the body of the faithful, the church. So it is the logic of
exemplification, itself a variant of *complementarity,* that deserves
closer scrutiny.

Years ago an astute layperson responded to a friend's wonder-
ment at priesthood—indeed at *his* priesthood—by reminding him
that he was a priest because we all are priests. It took him some
time to grasp the profundity of that statement and the logic it suggested peculiar to the church and sacraments: All followers of
Jesus are knit into a body that is a "royal priesthood," as Peter
quotes Exodus 19:5 (1 Pt 2:9). Yet that royal priesthood in which
the whole body shares will be realized by all only if it is con-
cretely embodied in some members. (This is the same logic that
gradually gave a kind of primacy to the see of Rome, with its
bishop embodying the unity of the *Catholica,* the worldwide

communion of faithful.) This is a dangerous logic, many would contend, though they might do so for quite different reasons. For some people it sounds too neat, like a simple apologia for sacerdotal (or Roman) primacy. For others such logic carries a hint of Donatism, since the notion of *exemplification* seems to entail that those fulfilling these offices ought to exemplify them in their personal lives. My response to the latter objection is that we can and must live with that much Donatism; and to the first, that a logic of exemplification (with its cognate complementarity) offers the best possible antidote to raw power. And we need such an antidote because otherwise secular models will inevitably impose themselves. None but the naive could want simply to import those into the community of faithful hoping that things will thereby improve.[11]

The church must indeed be ordered, but ordered in a way that exhibits the need of the ordained for laypersons, and also of men for women. As Newman is said to have once remarked when particularly piqued by clericalism: "The church would look very funny without the laity!" Correlatively, churches expressly without ordination soon come to delegate certain functions to particular members—to those, in fact, perceived to embody them already in their lives and character. The debate about ordination between "free church" and "mainline" models is probably unresolvable; both sides recognize the logic of exemplification, but seek different ways to execute it. And perhaps, like many salient interfaith differences, this disagreement needs to remain as a reminder that we will never fully understand such things, and so need different models to keep our respective practices in line with the gospel.

The test and fruit of our suggested way of understanding hierarchy will be the manner in which ordained and laity interact, the mutual appreciation each shows for the other, and ways in which the logic of exemplification works out in practice. Such is the challenge to the Christian community, and while failures make headlines, we can also testify to the fruitfulness of practices that work. In so doing, we confirm the prescient statement to my friend: You are a priest because we are all priests.

This novel yet biblical notion of *hierarchy* allows the people of God—lay as well as ordained—to work together for the good of the whole. Indeed, nothing is more characteristic of a genuine Christian community than a kind of symbiosis between priest and people. And nothing gives the lie to the standard caricature of *hierarchy* better than this fact of experience. For if all members of the community are concerned with being first only by serving, then the way everyone's gifts are exercised becomes more important than determining who has the power. Explicit ecclesiastical pronouncements may be concerned with explaining how and why holy orders ranks above matrimony, but ordained ministers who experience a fruitful life find such discourse irrelevant and insulting. If anything, they are inclined to appreciate the ways in which matrimony might be said to rank first. For their own experience will confirm the exhortation from the ritual for baptism: "Parents are the first and primary teachers of the faith to their children." What could top that role in shaping both church and society?

Christian married couples have tended to honor the significance of holy orders, often to the point of undervaluing that of matrimony. But there is hope that mutual respect for the meaning of each sacrament and collaborative responsibility for the welfare of the people of God could change that. Indeed, a theology revitalized by a new way of understanding the mission of Jesus can contribute to such a change. But only the Spirit can accomplish it. Given the power of the Spirit, however, those in holy orders would come to appreciate the "holy ordering" that matrimony embodies. They, along with the married themselves, will see how the sacrament of matrimony connects human beings to creation in an explicit way. It reminds us all of Jesus' mission to restore God's original order and of our call to participate in that restoration.

6

A WAY TO RESTORE CREATION

So far our explicit question is a Christian one: how to integrate faith in God's free creation of the universe with our redemption in Jesus. We discovered that Christianity's elaborated faith in the story of redemption needs to be connected with our notional belief in the universe as God's creation. That connection is necessary, in fact, if we are to appreciate creation itself as God's initial free gift. Moreover, we cannot even understand creation apart from God's self-giving in revelation. For Christians, that revelation comes in the life and work of Jesus, while for Muslims, as we noted, its locus is the unanticipated gift of an Arabic Qur'an. We have seen that a "new story" or a "creation perspective" that overlooks that of revelation is not what is needed for Christian theology, but rather a stereoscopic vision of what is already revealed. In short, we should regard creation and redemption as twin foci for our theological reflection. If we can exploit the interaction between them, then the graciousness of God will be more adequately revealed.

It is understandable that theologians have been searching for a way to highlight creation as God's primordial gift. We have noted how powerful forces conspired within Christianity to let the second article of the creed eclipse the first. While liturgical displacement of the Sabbath by the Lord's day may have exerted the greatest influence in practice, it was not the most theologically significant of these factors. That, doubtless, was the introduction of the domain of *grace* as an entitatively *supernatural* realm where human beings share a life with God. From a Christian perspective, the arguments for introducing such a realm are powerful. Henri deLubac's masterful analysis of the way baroque theology transposed the notion into a two-story universe certainly cleared the way for a more authentic understanding of *supernatural.*[1] Yet the issues surrounding the term remain problematic. So let us review those difficulties as a prelude to seeing how interfaith discussion can illuminate them even further.

DeLubac effectively employed a patristic perspective to show how baroque Thomists had distorted Aquinas's arguments supporting the need for a supernatural realm of grace. So Aquinas's authority cannot be invoked to support their position, although they did indeed invoke it. These theologians introduced a novelty into the tradition—one that would become as disastrous as it was commonplace. Their specific innovation was to come up with an entirely theoretical entity called "pure nature," whose finality was restricted to the domain of the human (however that might be defined). Their purpose in postulating this "nature" was laudable enough: to preserve the gratuity of God's gift of friendship to human beings. But to accomplish this end they insisted that the very capacity for such an unimaginable gift had to be created afresh by God and presented to us as something "extra." Were that not the case, they reasoned, then the opening in our limitless nature to personal union with God would *ipso facto* constrain God to grant that to which human beings aspired. Redemption, therefore, would cease to be a free gift.

Notice how easily this argument is generated once the natural/supernatural distinction is allowed to obscure the datum of revelation that our natures are *already* a gift of the creator. When that is lost sight of, however, human nature can be treated as a mere "fact of nature." Aristotle was comfortable with that way of thinking, but it is quite unrelated to God's revealed plan.[2] Nor does that way of understanding human nature represent the patristic perspective native to Aquinas. For him, rather, it is the same God who redeems as creates, and who creates us "from the beginning" with a view to friendship. And this means that the very openness of our natures to such an unimaginable end becomes part of what defines us as human beings. We can conclude, then, that being made in the "image and likeness of God," as revelation tells us, is what grants to our natures the transcendence that makes it impossible to characterize our *telos*.

Jean-Paul Sartre's insistence that human beings "have no nature" was, in fact, his dramatic way of making an analogous point. We are unable to circumscribe human nature by stating its proper goal, which (as Aristotle taught us) is one of the ways to define natures. In other words, what defines us is that we defy definition. Sartre would say that is simply how we are. Believers can conclude that that is how our natures were created to be. DeLubac concurred with Sartre in reminding us that a purely philosophical treatment of human nature is inadequate. And the further direction of Sartre's own thought suggests that a complete account of human nature will have to be theological—even if one's theology is an *atheology*.[3] John Milbank makes this same point in a more positive vein in his recent *Theology and Social Theory*. Canvassing the thinkers who have shaped modern discussions of the human, particularly Marx and Freud, Milbank shows how each one only *asserts* what he presents as the *telos* proper to human beings, thus demanding that readers take these assertions on faith. Indeed, there seems to be no other way, since human nature defies definition. But Milbank's masterful thesis yields a paradoxical result: The very accounts that purport to replace revelation with more accessible *scientific* perspectives turn out to be crypto-theologies themselves.[4]

The baroque Thomists, in attempting to develop a "purely philosophical" account of human nature, were not so different from later thinkers who touted a "scientific" one. These eighteenth-century

Thomists wanted to meet the intellectual world of their day by formulating a philosophical explanation of the cosmos shorn of extraneous data from revelation concerning the origin of the universe and the distinguishing characteristics of the human species. In an effort to speak to a wider world where the premises of faith were no longer shared, they created a split reality that would come to be called "the two-story universe." The effect this would have on the larger world was catastrophic. Religion became identified with the "supernatural" and faith could conveniently be regarded as an "extra." So human nature could be fulfilled without either. Moreover, their natural/supernatural distinction created a chasm between the first two articles of the creed, effectively annulling the first. The baroque theologians assigned creation and such matters to philosophy, while the wider culture presumed they belong to science.[5] No wonder, then, that these theologians were preoccupied with the "gratuity of grace," as they were wont to put it, oblivious of the redundancy. They had neatly overlooked the gratuity of creation—the first grace! This oversight separated philosophy from theology, and nature from grace, thereby yielding a spirituality with no roots in God's creation.

Another factor that worked to eclipse the first article of the creed was the nineteenth-century separation of history from nature. This bifurcation tended to leave nature to scientific inquiry and direct the attention of theologians to history, especially "salvation history," when looking for the action of God. Coupled with the dominantly "supernatural" spirituality issuing from baroque theology, the clean separation of history from nature proved a formidable obstacle to valuing the theological implications of creation. Eventually the call would come for a "new story"—indeed, one that would eclipse redemption as a way of restoring creation! The obvious antidote to such problems is to restore nature to the perspective of faith, where it properly belongs. The two gratuities of creation and redemption can then be adopted as the twin foci of Christian theology, thereby transforming the theological circle into an ellipse. But how? How take the first step of bringing the gratuity of creation into focus for Christians? This is precisely where interfaith dialogue offers a way. Such dialogue can help Christians (and, of course, Jews and Muslims as well) to clarify what we believe. Moreover, genuine dialogue among members of different traditions makes friendship possible, and no one can journey alone in the quest for self-discovery or in the effort to understand other religious traditions.

Exploring the way in which Jewish and Muslim religious thought contrasts with the supernatural will prove helpful, since neither ever developed a strong entitative account of God's redeeming action that Christians call "grace." Yet each of these traditions is drawn to explain the effective presence of the divine in our lives, a presence that flows from God's gratuitous creative activity. It is, of course, the free gift of the Torah and the Qur'an (each offering a *way* or a "straight path" to God) that manifests God's guiding presence. For both Jews and Muslims, the very possibility of such a presence is traced to the gratuitous activity of creation. It is precisely this free creation of the universe by a God who does not need to create that for them accounts for God's presence in revelation. From a comparative perspective, the challenging question is whether that revelation is liberating in a sense comparable to Christian redemption narratives. My spontaneous answer would be yes, yet the weight of interfaith polemics, as we shall see, moves against it.

A participant in interfaith dialogue as astute as Ewert Cousins insists that Islam has no archetype of transformation, whereas one is central to Christianity, whose doctrine of redemption has its roots in the Exodus experience of the Jews. He goes on to argue that while this archetype is basic to the Jewish and Christian reading of history, "Islam's view of history is grounded much more directly in God's power and providence without discerning a primordial pattern of transformation in the cosmos and in history."[6] Cousins wants to remind us how we must "pass over" from our own religious tradition to another without presuming similarities; indeed, we need to be aware of such functional archetypes precisely to discover the creative differences.[7] So far, so good; yet Cousins asserts that the transformation archetype functions in relation to history within Judaism and Christianity, but not in Islam. What his analysis misses, however, is a treatment in any of the three traditions of this archetype in relation to the cosmos! Islam could have offered some instances of the transformation archetype at work in the Qur'an's approach to creation. It is constantly reminding skeptics that the One who needs only to say "'Be' and it is" (2:117) will certainly have no difficulty raising all of us from the dead for a final judgment (50:11, 15).

Sufi thinkers, moreover, seem to have come intuitively to an insight cognate with Aquinas's statement (in ST 1.8.1) that nothing is more intimate to things than their very existing, which comes directly from the creator. (The Qur'an will say that the creator is "nearer to [man] than his jugular vein" (50:16).) Developments in Sufism, notably in Ibn al-Arabi but implicitly in many earlier witnesses, suggest that a "transformation archetype" is not so much absent as redundant. For them, God's creative action is intimately present to each human action, and indeed to every event in the universe. Perhaps that is what Cousins has in mind in saying that "Islam's view of history is grounded much more directly in God's power and providence." In any case, the Qur'an and subsequent Sufi traditions point away from "archetypal analysis" toward leading Christians to connect what we say about redemption with what we believe about creation, and vice-versa. If Christians (and Jews) were to follow that direction, a genuine "passing over and returning" could occur. For in the process of recognizing how well Islam functions without what we considered our organizing principle of thought, we Christians might notice a lacuna in a characteristic mode of doing theology. Realizations of this sort can be more heartening than threatening; they can enhance our awareness of the limitations to any theological approach. Furthermore, we could be reminded how ways of doing theology are inevitably influenced by fashions in thought, as is Cousins's, "phenomenological analysis of religions."

Archetypal analysis is not unlike other recent strategies developed to study "religion"—approaches that are a secularized residue of the chasm confirmed in baroque theology between *natural* and *supernatural.* What they study is invariably a product of human ingenuity or need (or whatever). The centrality of "redemption" in such schemes is a telling clue that religion begins and ends with human aspirations rather than being rooted in the wider universe. It can be argued that our preoccupation with *redemption* has effectively skewed our discussions of other faiths, which have followed upon our "discovering" them.[8] Beyond a redemptive one, any other function for religion would be tantamount to its presenting a "worldview." But that function—let us not forget—belongs not to religion but to philosophy. So the divisions of baroque theology prevail! And how can we avoid that? By insisting, as the triform creed does, that One who reveals a way is the very one who creates all-that-is. Then the redemption that revelation inevitably brings need not suggest a free-floating archetype for human aspirations, but can be parsed as "restoring the original order of God's creation."

The original order is presented mythically in the Hebrew scriptures as a verdant garden where God walked with human beings. In the Qur'an, that order is described as a primordial encounter in which God offers us "the trust" (33:72) of fulfilling our God-given natures by expressly returning all that has been given—indeed, the universe—to the One who freely bestows it. The fact that we let down our side of this original covenant did not necessitate the further bestowal of the Qur'an, of course. But our refusal of responsibility clearly defines its goal: to offer the "warning and guidance" needed for us to take up the defining human task and fulfill it. Thus the purpose of the "coming down" of the Qur'an in Islam is structurally identical with the "sending" of the Son in Christianity—to offer us a *way* to follow in restoring the original order of God's creation. And in both revelations, because creation emanates freely from the One, human beings are given a free gift inviting a free response. Accepting the challenge not only promises "salvation," but unites the respondent with the entire universe. From the Muslim perspective, in giving the Qur'an as the way of salvation, God entrusts believers with a task analogous to the original "trust," but not precisely the same. For now the task is daunting beyond measure. Our aboriginal refusal entails that the order cannot simply be returned; the very effort to return the gift must be able to restore the original order in our wholeheartedly returning it to its giver.

Here is where the Christian teaching on "original sin" is more realistic than the often polemical Muslim denial of it. Muslims, on the whole, are no better or worse than Christians in fulfilling the trust, although the Qur'an gives them a "straight path." Even where the preaching of God's Word has overcome a prevailing ignorance *[jâhilîyya]*, it can scarcely be said that a polity is established in which all who call themselves Muslims now fulfill the divine trust. So something must be at work—something that allows even believers to resist God's creating and revealing Word as it calls them to return all things to the One who bestows them. Sufi teaching explicitly adverts to this fact by elaborating a rich doctrine of grace, illustrated by the path *[tarîqa]* to holiness, which is marked by distinct *stations* and assisted by God-given *states*.[9] These two notions function like *virtues* and *gifts of the Holy Spirit* in Christian theology. In both Islam and Christianity, each modification of the human condition complements the other to show how the believer can live a life whose demands will often exceed human capacities. Yet such demands are always in service of a promise—of life lived in proximity to God—that responds to what is most human in our aspirations. Stations are settled ways of acting and responding to which we can attain, and on which we subsequently rely. This is precisely Aristotle's notion of a *virtue*. States refer to an explicitly divine influence effecting transformations that facilitate acting and responding in ways quite beyond our own expectations. Christian theology calls them "gifts of the Holy Spirit," for they cannot be predicted or relied upon since they may be given for a particular purpose and only for a specific time. The teachings of both religious traditions are remarkably similar on these points.[10]

What is essential here is that some divine assistance—whether continuing or transitory—will be required. For the Qur'an that is necessary for human beings to execute the "trust" originally given by God. For the New Testament, assistance is needed to participate in Jesus' mission of restoring the original divine order. The faiths may differ on how much they emphasize the "supernatural" character of this assistance; there are even differences among Christian theological traditions on this score. But in all of them, divine assistance is requisite. The more we reflect on this, the more useful is the notion of the *supernatural* to underscore the interpersonal character of the relation between believers and their God. Among Muslims, the preferred expression for a faithful person is "servant of God" [*'abd-Allah* or Abdullah], indicating someone who has ceased to serve selfish interests and is intent on making "the return" to God. Nonetheless, Sufis spontaneously speak of becoming God's friend *[walî]*. In a similar manner, on the eve of his passion Jesus announces to his disciples: "I no longer will call you 'servants' but 'friends'" (Jn 15:15). In both cases, friendship denotes a special form of attachment; it need not be construed as introducing an entitatively supernatural order. Yet God does call some to a more intimate union, and we must have a way of expressing that.

Since the One who is creator can initiate any relationship, there is no problem from God's side. But friendship with God will require something to facilitate a commensurate response on the creature's part. This is the logic that motivated the natural/supernatural distinction in Christian theology, which seems harmless enough so long as the human response is understood to be responding to the initiative of a free creator. What made the distinction destructive was a theology that no longer regarded the creature's free response as directed to its creator, but had already severed redemption from creation by speaking of "two orders." That sort of language is in no way entailed by distinguishing *supernatural* from *natural*. Prior to baroque theology, *supernatural* simply called attention to the quality of intimacy that God extends to those who are faithful. The use of the term, therefore, should be restricted to that call to friendship with God. Since Christian theology at its best, however, has always presumed a formal analogy among creation, incarnation, and sanctification, it would be natural to fashion the "new creation" of the faithful on the hard-earned characterization of Jesus as two natures—divine and human—united in the person of God's eternal Word.

Interfaith exchange can also offer Christians a fresh perspective on the role of Jesus as *mediator*. In the face of theories of the atonement that emphasize the need for Jesus' death as a sacrifice to set things right, Islam (and others) can justly ask: Why should the One who creates all-that-is immediately by a simple Word need a mediator to gain access to creatures? Those who formulated the theories would respond that it is not God but we who need the mediator, given the alienation effected by our sin. But these theologians never answered why God would then demand the bloody sacrifice of his only Son! Could not the creator of heaven and earth just set things right? We have already seen that the answer to that question is no, but the account given (with credits to Sebastian Moore) lies beyond the ken of satisfaction theories: It focuses on the need that *we* have for a victim to bring us to our collective and individual senses.[11] Yet given the damage done by such theories, can the notion of Jesus as mediator be refurbished? Indeed it can, by recovering the patristic perspective that antedated such theories, especially the theology of Leo the Great. He returned in his sermons again and again to the union of the divine and human natures in the person of the Word, which kept the natures distinct from one another. In Leo's hands, this very union offers Christians a unique way of characterizing the relation of creation to creator, so Jesus' being *mediator* has nothing to do with some status "between" God and creatures. It is rather that the very structure of the union of human and divine natures in Jesus brings God and creatures together in a new way.

So a developed doctrine of the incarnation offers Christians a way of articulating what escapes human conceptual skills: the relation of creator to creation. We will be able to see this more clearly by returning to a teaching that Christianity shares with Judaism and Islam: the *oneness* of God. That central doctrine certainly cannot be reduced to the observation that these three all insist there is numerically only one God, while other religions postulate more than one. *Oneness* does not refer to number but to the nature of divinity. And that turns on creation: This God in whom Jews, Christians, and Muslims believe is the one creator of all-that-is, so that no created thing can be "associated" with this One (Qur'an 6:22). Rabbinic teaching on divine *unity* finds its counterpart in Islamic *tawhid* or "faith in divine unity." Both traditions are making a religious point embodied in the prohibition against idolatry or *shirk* (that is, *associating* others with God), as well as a philosophical point that has been nicely stated by Robert Sokolowski as "the distinction" of God from the world.[12] And it can be argued that it took four centuries to formulate the doctrine of the incarnation at Chalcedon (in 451) because Christians needed time to show *themselves* that they were not idolaters in believing what they did about Jesus.[13] The final conceptual clarification of "two natures in one [divine] person" permitted an unequivocal confession of faith in Jesus as the unique creator-creature. Unlike what some philosophers had implied, the doctrinal formula boldly proclaimed that Jesus was not some "third thing" *between* creator and creature, but the unparalleled instance of one who was *both.* Such an understanding of Jesus as mediator offers Christianity a singular advantage in doing what all three Abrahamic faiths must do: attempt to express the relation of creator to creation. That is beyond what human language can express, but the incarnation provides the best analogy for how to try.

During the Middle Ages, thinkers from each of the three traditions had to contend with a prevailing cosmological scheme of necessary emanation from the One. Al-Ghazali, Moses Maimonides, and Thomas Aquinas all had to work against this elegant conceptual structure to preserve God's freedom in creating, and struggle they did.[14] In exposing the seductive power of an emanation scheme that linked creation to a grand logical system, these thinkers helped us to realize that the relation of creator to creation escapes human formulation. They also pointed out that factors contributing to the ineffability of that relation are its freedom and its immediacy. God does not need to create and did so with a sovereign freedom; nor does God need any assistance in creating, so accomplishes it immediately. These primarily religious affirmations called forth a set of philosophical strategies more sophisticated than the logical model of emanation. The key move was introduced by Ibn Sina (Avicenna) and quickly adopted and adapted both by Moses Maimonides and Thomas Aquinas: distinguishing the fact-*that*-something-is from *what*-it-is. Once that distinction is made, *existing* becomes much more than a *fact;* it is the source of all activity and hence of any perfections a thing can claim. Aquinas was led to assert that the very "to-be of things is the proper effect" of the creator in creating and for that very reason none but God, the One whose essence is simply to-be, can create; intermediaries would be utterly redundant (ST 1.45.5).

While this shared effort succeeded admirably in securing "the distinction" of God from creatures, it was less felicitous in formulating their manner of being related—except to insist that creation is immediate and never mediated. Difficulties were inevitable; where a distinction is formulated without articulating the complementary relation, the human tendency will be to characterize the resulting "objects" over against one another. In other words, distinguishing between two things easily turns them into two separate objects. In the case at hand, that way of thinking certainly threatens the unique status of God as creator. For the single thing we know about this One is that it is *not* one of those "things" whose source and goal it constitutes (ST 1.2. Prol). Yet the moment we characterize God "over against" the universe, we have turned the creator into one of those things![15] On the other hand, to articulate the unique relatedness of that One to whatever exists as the "nonduality" of God and the universe appears to annihilate the all-important "distinction." What is crucial about the distinction in the three traditions is the way it secures God's freedom in creating. But does not that very freedom mean that the universe "adds nothing" to God, and so assure that it cannot be *separate* from the One?

No wonder Islamic thinkers parted on this issue. Those intent on trying to formulate the relatedness of God to God's servants would find themselves drawn to speaking of an "inner relatedness" that might easily be thought to confuse creature with creator. That was certainly the case with the early mystic al-Hallaj, and even more so in the elaborations of Ibn al-Arabi.[16] On the other side, those concerned to secure the distinction between creator and creatures would inevitably seem to render the God of the Qur'an remote. To be sure, the principal reason for such oscillation in Islamic thought is that the relation of creator to creature defies conceptualization. In fact, what we have been calling "the distinction" and "an inner relatedness" translates into traditional conundra regarding God's transcendence and immanence.

We can now return to the incarnation and appreciate how it sheds light on the creator/creature relation. The ontological constitution of Jesus, called the "hypostatic union," offers a unique instance of a being who embodies this mysterious relation in his own person. And while that will not bring us any closer to a satisfactory formulation of the relation itself, it does seem to quiet the sort of oscillation we have noted in Islamic thinkers. For Christians can see in Jesus a paradigm embodying the distinction and an inner relatedness in a single person. What remains mysterious is the manner of their union in this person and, of course, the *person* itself. We have come to see how linking the mission of Jesus to creation sheds light on creation itself in ways that would be inaccessible without the teaching of the incarnation. Recognizing these connections should quiet further calls for a "new story" that pretends to uncover creation by obscuring redemption. Indeed, in the measure that the Christian tradition has effectively eclipsed creation by focusing unilaterally on redemption, a distortion can hardly be corrected by reversing it! Instead, we have been proposing a twin focus on creation and redemption that allows one to illuminate the other, for both are matters of faith.

Our guide has been a remark by Aquinas that could be taken as summing up his reflection on these delicate matters. It is also the fruit of his struggle—along with Maimonides and Ghazali—to formulate the freedom of God's creation in which Christians believe. Aquinas's remark is virtually hidden in the response to an objection in the passage asking "whether the trinity of divine persons can be known by natural reason" (ST 1.32.1.3). His answer to that question is of course no, since the path from creatures to God will not yield any insight into the inner life of God. Moreover, it is an abuse of reason to pretend to prove what can be known only by faith, a strategy that can bring only ridicule on those who try it. He also says the same for anyone who seeks to prove that creation occurred at an initial moment of time—something that indicted his co-religionist Bonaventure, as well as Muslim religious thinkers *[mutikallimun]* (ST 1.46.1). Yet Aquinas goes on to respond to an odd objection: that it would be superfluous to teach what cannot be known by natural reason. Far from being superfluous, he argues, "knowledge of the divine persons was necessary for us [if we are to have] the right idea of creation:...saying that God made all things by His Word excludes the error of those who say that God produced things by necessity;

[and] when we say that in Him there is a procession of love, we show that God produced creatures not because He needed them, nor because of any other extrinsic reason, but on account of the love of His own goodness" (ST 1.32.1.2). So the revelation of God in Jesus, elaborated into the doctrine of the triune God— Father, Son [Word], and Holy Spirit—yields a fresh perspective on creation as an utterly free act. This God is constrained neither by necessity of nature nor by need for fulfillment; such a One can create only out of love.[17] Furthermore, the verse from Wisdom, "the Spirit of the Lord has filled the world / and that which holds all things together knows what is said" (1:7), is rendered more explicit when the Spirit is identified as "a procession of love." Here again, Aquinas's perspective, along with that of major Sufi thinkers, is striking. They center on the Qur'anic verse: "God will bring a people whom He loves and who love Him…; such is the grace *[fadl]* of God which He gives to whom He will" (5:54). Among the myriad verses of the Qur'an, Sufis focus on this one because the mention of love and grace completes another verse, the frequently stated "God has only to say 'Be' and it is" (2;117, 3:47, 57; 6:73, 16:40, 19:35, 36:82, 40:68). We are reminded that God need not have said anything at all! The original "trust" was offered by God as a sign of love, while those who set out whole-heartedly to fulfill it will be responding to love, rather than acting out of duty or constraint. This is the inner logic of a free creation on the part of One who has shown the compassion of "sending down…a clear light [to] guide those who believe in God to Himself by a straight path" (4:175).

So whether we are speaking of Christianity or of Islam, it is the revelation of God that invariably leads us to recognize the true face of the creator. Signs may abound in the universe, but revelation alone offers the clues for interpreting them properly. In fact, the word for *signs* in Arabic—*ayât*—is the same word for *verses* in the Qur'an, a way of reminding us that we will begin to recognize the signs of creation once we allow ourselves to be instructed by the palpable signs of God's spoken word. Augustine implies something parallel in his *Confessions*. For it is not until the tenth book, well after his wholehearted response to the living Word of God, that he inquires of "earth,...sea, the deeps, the living creatures that creep, [and] with a great voice they cried out: 'He made us' (Ps. 99:3)"(10.5). And their response is not only a cosmological statement, for he initiates his inquiry by asking: "What is the object of my love?" Having found that "object" in the Word made flesh and articulated in the scriptures, he can now hear creatures insist that "we are not your God, look beyond us" as well as remind him that "He made us."

7

THE CREATOR AND CREATION

How can we begin to articulate the elusive relation of creator to creation? The initial cause of all-that-is cannot be thought of as just one more item in the universe. As Kathryn Tanner reminded us, never attempt to speak of divinity in terms that simply contrast God with the universe.[1] Yet a way opened up during an interview for a position in comparative religions with a candidate who was offering an account of what is called in Vedanta "nondualism." As Bradley Malkovsky—now our colleague at Notre Dame—delineated Vedanta teaching on this unique relation of the universe to its origin it dawned on me: Nondualism is an attempt to state positively what Kathryn Tanner puts negatively. And so, that would offer one more example of the way in which encountering another tradition can help to disentangle a misunderstanding that bedevils a particular tradition.

In other words, is the difference between believers and unbelievers simply that believers hold that there is one more item in the universe than nonbelievers—namely, God? Assertive theists often talk that way; reflective believers find the question puzzling if not offensive. Thomas Aquinas suggests why when he opens his *Summa Theologiae* by locating the object of his inquiry as "the beginning and end of all things, and of reasoning creatures especially" (ST 1.2. Prol). Asserting that God is the source of all-there-is, therefore, also means that God is the end or goal of all creatures. Yet it is precisely those creatures whose nature acts toward an end who illustrate how God is the end of all things. Given so pregnant an introduction to the topic of Aquinas's masterwork, the implication is evident: God is *not* one of those things that God originates. So whatever God may be said to be, for Aquinas God cannot simply be another item in the universe— however large or powerful. Reflections of this sort remind us why reflective believers seldom need to be disabused of a "God out there," for they have never conceived of God that way. Even if they have no idea *how* to conceive of divinity, they can recognize that any formulation aligning God with the universe itself cannot be taken seriously. Augustine's *Confessions* offers the classical locus for such reflection: that work presents a perennial source for discovering patterns that present themselves to seekers who struggle to find appropriate ways of speaking of divinity.

To return to the recurring theme of our work, when Christian theologians speak of a redeemer and lose sight of the grounding relation of the universe to its creator, God will be introduced as the one who "comes to save us." Given the palpable presence of Jesus as a human individual "sent by God," moreover, Christians will misconceive God as initially separate from the universe, but now entering into it in the incarnation. Correlatively, the relation between Jesus and "the Father" will be pictured as an interaction between two distinct individuals. This tendency has generated the bizarre formulations we can find in certain "atonement theories," which posit Jesus' death as a way of offering "satisfaction" to God for our sins! Such distortions do not follow ineluctably from neglecting the original and originating relation of creation, of course, but that neglect makes it easier to postulate a "God out there" who is the agent of "our salvation." We have already noted that in the Christian tradition the effort to formulate the unique relation that is creation finds expression in the internal relation between the divine and human natures of Jesus. We shall now explore how reformulating that original relation as *nondualism* offers a perspicuous way of understanding the assertions of Chalcedon articulating Christ's constitution as two natures in one divine person.

It was a small book by Sara Grant, R.S.C.J., entitled *Towards an Alternative Theology: Confessions of a Non-dualist Christian,* that helped me to articulate the insight that dawned while hearing my colleague speak of Sankara.[2] Sara Grant speaks with the authority of someone trained in Indian philosophy as well as practiced in a life given over to bringing the conceptualities and practices of East and West into fruitful interaction. In the book she describes her move from an early unease with the blatantly dualist presentation of Christianity as a redemptive scheme to her growing sense of fruitful complementarity between the original teaching of Sankara and Aquinas's formulation of the relation of the universe to its creator. Eventually she would affirm that "a non-reciprocal relation of dependence…, far from diminishing the uniqueness and lawful autonomy of a created being within its own sphere, was their necessary Ground and condition, while apart from that relation of total dependence no created being would *be* at all."[3] Sara Grant's capacity for recognizing that conceptual complementarity developed during her early formation in contemplative prayer under a wise novice mistress of the Society of the Sacred Heart in England. This woman planted the living seed that would demand an appropriate form of expression in a spirit as consequent as that of Sara Grant. Being sent to India initially confronted the young sister as a challenge in obedience, for she had asked to go to Brazil (after completing "Greats" at Oxford and teaching for six years in a Sacred Heart school), yet that move proved to be her conceptual salvation.

And she surely needed salvation of that sort, since her prescient novice mistress had died as superior of their house at Oxford during Sara Grant's tenure there. Soon she would be told by the Society's highest authority to "forget all [your] Mistress of Novices had taught [you] and trust the spirituality of the Society"—a spirituality whose nineteenth-century formulations (still regnant in 1948) could only rankle the young sister-philosopher.[4] Yet something within her reached for the crucial distinction between "substance and formulation" with which John XXIII was to introduce Vatican Council II. And Sara Grant continued along the way she had been led by her novice mistress, fueled by the conviction that "the Eternal underpinned and permeated everything, and that was enough."[5] While this formulation came retrospectively, it captures the intuitive nondualism that would lead her on the search for an explicit one. But just how does she (and how can we) formulate this elusive notion? As the term suggests, it reaches for a middle ground between *dualism* and *monism*. *Nondualism* mediates two proclivities: on the one hand, the tendency to treat the relation of the universe to its origin as one between two distinct entities—if not on the same plane at least comparable in ordinary discourse (dualism); on the other hand, considering the universe merely as expression of its originative source, so that there is no *relation* between them (monism). What the middle ground *nondualism* seeks to express is a relation of a unique kind, reflecting the unique "distinction" between the universe and its source. So this conceptualization itself affirms the unique ontological status of the One.[6]

Regarding this matter, Sufi thinkers preferred to remind us that if everything has its origin and its continuing sustenance in God, nothing can be *outside* of God! For anything to be at all, therefore, its very being must be dependent on the creator. It is our responsibility to seek for ways of expressing that, especially because the ordinary path of ignorance *[jâhilîyya],* or of *illusion* (Sankara), presumes that we exist autonomously, in our own right. Islam's experience early on with the Mu'tazilite school, which had no way of securing human freedom except to withdraw the entire domain of human actions from the creator's activity, alerted Muslim thinkers to the danger of opposing creator to creature.[7] (Mu'tazilite thinkers took this bizarre position because they could imagine only a single sense for "acting," which was tantamount to "creating." So if actions were to be attributed to us, we would have to be their creators.) Speaking out of the Indian traditions, Sara Grant insists that "nondualism is not merely a matter of intellectual conviction: it consists also in an existential experience, confirming intellectual convictions of the absolute transcendence-in-immanence of the ultimate Mystery in relation to all that exists or occurs at the relatively ephemeral level of 'ordinary' life."[8] That experience she expresses as "a kind of wordless and conceptless adherence to the truth of one's own being which, however obscure and painful, is also strangely liberating." That inner sustenance had carried her through childhood, into religious life, and through the misunderstandings present there. Such experience gestures toward a *presence-in-absence* that not a few of us have known.

Sara Grant's primary concern was to understand Vedanta, and early in her search she found that the "potted" accounts that conveyed what was retailed to the West—that the world we live in is but "illusion"—were not fruitful. She began a "study of nondualism *[advaita]* in the light of the commentaries of Sankarâcârya,"[9] and taking the advice of the Belgian Jesuit authority on Sankara, Richard DeSmet, she focused on the concept of relation. This proved to be a valuable cross-cultural tool, given the key role relation plays in Thomas Aquinas's attempts to formulate "the distinction" of God from the world as well as the *distinctions* within a triune God. Sara Grant soon found that the commentary tradition in India had all but obscured Sankara's original thought, while the work of L. Krempel on "the doctrine of relation in Aquinas" showed how that Western thinker had been visited with a similar fate.[10] So a parallel task of "deconstruction" to uncover the thought of these original thinkers was to lead her to the kind of mutual illumination that cross-cultural experience and study so often elicits. As she puts it in summary fashion: "For both Sankara and Thomas, Being and being are not one in an absolutely monistic sense, as a man and his shadow are not one, but they are not absolutely two either, for each could have made his own the statement of the 14th century English Mystic [author of the *Cloud of Unknowing*]: 'He is thy Being but thou are not his being.'"[11] Sheer origination can be accurately rendered only as "a non-reciprocal relation of dependence."[12] James Ross's pregnant image comes to mind: "The universe is related to its creator as the song on the lips of a singer."[13]

The mutual illumination of comparative analysis offers fresh light to both sides. Sara Grant reminds us that for Thomas, "the flowing-out *(emanation)* and return of creatures from and to God their Source and end [is] enfolded in the 'coming forth' and 'returning' of the eternal Word in whom all things were created and continue to subsist."[14] So the creation of the universe follows the pattern of the generation of the Word in God, eternally established. That very pattern is revealed by the One "who himself 'became flesh' and dwelt as a man among men, 'for the life of the world.'" And the mission of the incarnate Word is, as we have seen, to restore the original order of God's creation. Both creation and redemption, as God's free activity, lie quite beyond our ken, but treated in isolation from one another, they become utterly unintelligible. And if we fail to keep in focus the originating relation of creation, inevitably we will speak dualistically of God *and* the universe. Nevertheless, the Christian community's experience with Jesus—who came to be understood as the incarnate Word of God—yielded a rich trinitarian theology, allowing us to root creation itself in the eternal procession within divinity of that same Word "though whom all things are made." The redemptive work of Jesus the Christ, therefore, returns us to creation in theory as well as in practice. Once again, our recurring theme emerges: The goal of Jesus' redemptive mission is best formulated as restoring God's original peace—the originating *order* of creation that is God's own Word.

Moreover, as we suggested earlier, the relation between divinity and humanity in Jesus will be "a particular and privileged Instance of the relationship established by the primordial act of creation."[15] And Sara Grant shows us how the nondualism expressed in "the non-reciprocal relation of *ananyatva*" can assist us with the conundrum of the incarnation. She formulates it succinctly: "How can a Godhead which can undergo no change whatever be united with a humanity which was to be devoid of any differentia which would make it less fully human than that of any other member of the human race?"[16] *Ananyatva* intends to express "a dependence so radical that the dependent reality cannot for a moment exist or act apart from its inner cause or Ground, which remains on its side wholly untouched by the relation." And this expresses the entire dynamic of the life of Jesus as we have come to know it: a life lived utterly "from the Father and to the Father" with "no tendency at all to claim a false autonomy." Claims to autonomy are precisely what turn created reality into illusion, and they express "the Hindu equivalent of original sin—*avidyá* or ignorance," which Sara Grant defines as "an existential kind of ignorance, a tendency to absolutize relatives and most disastrously the individual ego, [which] of course is complete illusion and total destruction."[17] It is fascinating to find here, as in Islam, an analogue to what Christians call "original sin," albeit within a frame of expression that is quite different. Yet once again, comparing them without attempting to reduce one to the other can only be illuminating for both traditions.

I have relied utterly on Sara Grant's presentation in her brief yet prescient Teape lectures, since I can claim no expertise whatsoever in Vedanta. In fact, when I began to familiarize myself with Islam nearly fifteen years ago, I did so convinced that one could no longer attempt theology in any form without doing it comparatively. Several personal factors inclined me to a study of Islam, among them my previous work in matters medieval, which called for a natural extension to that culture which had fertilized philosophical reflection in the West. That Muslims, along with Jews and Christians, averred the free creation of the universe by one God also drew me toward a study of Islam (after having paid considerable attention to Judaism and its internal relations with Christianity). What I then thought to be a pervasive equivocation regarding this primary relation of creation in Hinduism had also warned me away from it as a field of study. So it has been startling for me to discover how my subsequent struggles to understand the utter uniqueness of that relation could find expression in a conceptuality at the heart of Hindu thought. Such are the surprises of comparative study—almost at every corner!

8

THE END OF IT ALL

The world that T. S. Eliot had ending "not with a bang but a whimper" is more like the one we have created than the one God creates. Both Bible and Qur'an fasten on the cataclysmic character of the end, and while a good part of that scenario is linked to the final judgment humans will face, the signs and the effects are cosmic: "Look I am making the whole of creation new" (Rv 21:5); and "on the day when the blast convulses the world and there follows a blast yet again, on that Day all hearts will be filled with agitation and all eyes with dread" (Qur'an 79-6-9). Why must all of this be destroyed in order to introduce the "new creation"? A simple response would be: to assure that *all* of it is *new!* And that is certainly one way in which the literary genre of *apocalyptic* is used in both renditions. Yet the book of Revelation and the Hebrew prophets are equally concerned that the manifold injustices perpetrated by those holding power be exposed and the situation set aright. Similarly, the Qur'an continually excoriates those who live unmindful of its warnings, while promising a life of bliss to those who heed them. So the *newness* of the universe restored on "that day" will have to entail removing everything that refuses or fails to serve the ends for which it has been created: returning praise to the creator.

Only human beings can refuse their destiny, however, so their reversal will be that much more traumatic. So it could be that the recurring sense of disaster attending "that day" reflects the human response that suffuses both the Bible and the Qur'an. In any case, what is assured is that the whole of creation will be made new. But will all that happen only on "that day"? Must we simply be obedient to the way offered to us, and wait patiently for the doors to this new world to be thrown open at the time of our death and at the final judgment? Here is where the perspectives of the Sufis and the gospel of John emerge as filling a lacuna in the way the Qur'an or Jesus' teaching might be received. In both, life is understood as given in the revelation itself, and so new life has already begun for those who believe it in their hearts. Christian theology expresses this fact as a doctrine of *grace,* which became, at the hands of Thomas Aquinas, an "entitatively supernatural" realm. Thus the desire of human beings (made in the divine image to execute a wholehearted return to their creator) is at once confirmed and facilitated by an explicit share in the inner life of that same creator. The believer, therefore, is already initiated into the new creation. For Aquinas it is possible to say that the believer is, in fact, already living the life promised in the resurrection. That is precisely what we mean in speaking of the "entitatively supernatural": a robust doctrine of grace.

When the Word of God is believed to become human, such an assertion comes more easily than it does to Islam, where the Word becomes a Qur'an. Yet it is noteworthy that early on in Islamic life and practice the words of that book began to take flesh in the minds and hearts of those who recited them with faith. When we speak of a "Sufi perspective," that is what we mean. These Muslim believers had (and continue to have) recourse to certain key verses of the Qur'an to license their relating to the book in the way they do. Yet once the larger Islamic community had unequivocally affirmed that the Qur'an was indeed the uncreated Word of God, Sufi practice could be seen as simply a heartfelt response to that doctrine. Book though it is, the Qur'an presents itself as far more than a book. So there is a natural affinity for the mystical in both biblical and Qur'anic believers. Phrases such as Paul's "I am alive yet it is no longer I but Christ living in me" (Gal 2:20) are repeated in various of his letters, and expressly linked to the resurrection in Romans 8:11: "If the Spirit of him who raised Jesus from the dead has made his home in you, then he who raised Christ Jesus from the dead will give life to your own moral bodies through his Spirit living in you." And like so much in the New Testament, Paul's words simply put a fine point on Ezechiel's "I shall put my Spirit within you and you shall live" (37:14).

Here we can recognize one of the sources of the elaboration of Christian faith in a triune God—Father, Son, and Spirit. Sufis, however, discovered similar resources in a resolutely monotheistic Islam, through a practice of recollection *(dhikr)* of God's uncreated Word made Qur'an, which introduced them into the very life—or *spirit*—of the one God. Polemics would make this move suspect, of course, since such proximity to God carries echoes of Christian trinitarian faith. Nonetheless, this proclivity established itself at the very heart of Islam wherever it went. Moreover, some theological traditions within Christianity have been suspicious of so robust a doctrine of grace, fearing it to be too "metaphysical" or bordering on the mystical. But showing how such a doctrine of grace represents a living realization of the eschatological promises of Christianity (and of Islam), we can hope to make its inescapably "metaphysical" character less suspect. And its mystical penchant can also be seen to be thoroughly consonant with Jesus' mission to restore the original order of creation, for a journey that aligns seekers with the inner harmonies of the universe as they draw closer to God can only be called *mystical*. Indeed, such an inward alignment is precisely what most religious traditions mean by "mystical."

Surely that is how John of the Cross presents the spiritual journey.[1] And if that sounds paradoxical to those who know him only secondhand, it will resonate with anyone who grasps the point of John's emphasis on purification. And whoever appreciates him

first of all as a poet is best able to do just that. The rigorous train-
ing John of the Cross prescribes is intended to bring all of us to
the limpidity of vision that attends the poet in fleeting moments
of inspiration. "All of us" here means all the parts of each one of
us, and most notably our desire.[2] For what clouds our vision is
distorted desire—desire that reaches out for what will truly satisfy but settles for what it knows will not. It is our plight to be
idolaters in practice. John must offer exercises to test the level of
our attachment to idols precisely to liberate authentic desire for
the God we cannot see. In that regard, it is fascinating to note that
his examples of attachments tend to fall into the category of what
psychologists would call "projections": attitudes we assume
toward objects of desire that keep us from desiring them properly, or toward objects so construed as to be themselves improper.
Another person, for example, is never offered as an example of
an attachment, though our feelings toward other persons are often
cited. John of the Cross cannot be urged as an authority for so
unchristian a form of spirituality, which finds love for another
human being to be inimical to love for God. Things or attitudes
can block our access to God; other persons in themselves do not
pose an obstacle. Indeed, how could they, given Jesus' single
commandment, which John has passed on to us: "Love one
another as I have loved you"? But because projections do tend to
rule in ordinary intercourse among individuals, John's strictures
come into play. Purification of our projections constitutes the
path toward fulfilling Jesus' commandment.[3]

How can this account of the journey that John of the Cross presents corroborate our account of Jesus' mission as restoring the
original order of God's creation? Consider the penultimate stanza
of the *Spiritual Canticle*. There John is attempting to describe the
indescribable bliss of spiritual marriage: "What You gave me on
that other day." There we find five things "which she [the soul]
says the Bridegroom will bestow on her in that beatific transformation." They are contained in the stanza itself:

> The breathing of the air
> The song of the sweet nightingale,
> The grove and its living beauty
> In the serene night,
> With a flame that is consuming and painless

which John parses as follows:

> First, she says it is the breath of spiration of the Holy Spirit from God
> to her and from her to God.
> Second, that it is rejoicing the fruition of God.
> Third, that it is the knowledge of creatures and of their orderly
> arrangement.
> Fourth, that it is pure and clear contemplation of the divine essence.
> Fifth, that it is a total transformation in the immense love of God.[4]

Considering these five gifts accompanying the indescribable union of a person with God, we might legitimately be surprised to find the third. The others are obviously linked to "the spiritual life," but the third seems out of place. John associates it with the third line in the stanza: "the grove and its living beauty," in which he identifies the grove with God as the One who "nurtures and gives being to all creatures rooted and living in Him" who in this moment "shows Himself to her and reveals Himself as Creator." By the "living beauty" the person "intends to beg for the grace, wisdom, and beauty which every earthly and heavenly creature not only has from God but also manifests in its wise, well-ordered, gracious, and harmonious relationship to other creatures." Moreover, "the knowledge of this harmony fascinates and delights the soul."[5]

What is the point of this gift? There are many ways of putting it: to be able to see the world aright, to take pleasure in it as it comes from the hand of God, to delight in the "good of order" that reveals the giver in celebrating the gift, to return thanks to the Lord because we can finally see what a gift we have been given in the life we have received. The world is, in fact, ordered, yet our own rapacity keeps us from seeing what is before our faces. It might even be argued that John's third gift is on a par with the others—all concerned with God's immediacy—because the gift of life comes immediately from God to the "center of the soul." So the culminating chapters of the mature work of John of the Cross describing the indescribable final stage in one's progressive union with God return us to creation without any fanfare. John realizes full well that there are not "two stages" of gift, but only one: The world is created in the Word, the same Word who is made flesh. There is, moreover, the intimation that a person willing to follow Jesus all the way will be brought to grasp the point of parables like the "lilies of the fields." John is uncompromising, it is true, but he is so in all directions. The degree and quality of liberation of desire that he promises to those who can tolerate the darkness leaves us beholden to no one—but the Lord. That is true freedom and true appreciation of the gift of creation.

Connecting authentic freedom with appreciating the gift of creation offers us a fruitful tack for understanding John of the Cross in our interfaith, intercultural climate. One cannot visit the Iberian peninsula—Andalusia especially, but Toledo as well—without recognizing a culture whose perspectives were formed in an interchange among Jews, Christians, and Muslims. Miguel Asin Palacios has probed some of the connections in a slim work translated as *Saint John of the Cross and Islam.*[6] While his parallels may appear circumstantial to a historian, the fact of intercultural communication in Spain at the time of John is palpable. It is precisely this perspective of freedom that suggests a real communication. John stands firmly in the Augustinian tradition that insists *non est liber nisi liberatus:* We are not free unless we are freed. The background is our tendency to try to satisfy the divine restlessness within us with ersatz substitutes. The only cure is to allow God's grace the freedom to remake us according to the divine image already inscribed in our hearts by the creator. A recent essay by a Muslim contributor to a French symposium on the subject of freedom remarks that "freedom is essentially for Islam the liberation of the spirit."[7] For "man is essentially *'abd Allah,* the slave of God....Unless he is God's slave alone, man is fated to be the slave of others or of himself."[8] He remarks that the freedom that quite naturally appears to the West as a starting point is more readily understood in Islam as something to be attained by acceptance *(islam)* of the call that God gives to humankind. So freedom can never stand alone; it "should be seen as that necessary condition in which man can respond fully to the love of God."[9] As developed, it becomes utter "spontaneity in the act of cleaving to God" as evidenced in the Sufi mystics. Were John of the Cross to have picked up resonances of this teaching, which could easily have been transmitted in popular ballads (for Arab love poetry captures profound Qur'anic themes), it would have confirmed his Christian sense of our created divine image being restored by divine grace. Such an insight provides a vehicle for linking the goal of redemption to a renewed gratitude for creation.

Indeed, John's notorious ascetical maxims, prescribed at the outset of the journey, might well be understood as a way for seekers to escape the fearful cataclysm of the endtime. To submit to such thoroughgoing purification along the way is already to have come close to the end. After an extensive analysis of the vagaries of appetite, those intent on pursuing the "Ascent of Mount Carmel" are counseled to "endeavor to be inclined always":

> not to the easiest, but to the most difficult;
> not to the most delightful, but to the harshest;
> not to the most gratifying, but to the less pleasant;
> not to what means rest for you, but to hard work;
> not to the consoling, but to the unconsoling;
> not to the most, but to the least.[10]

And we are immediately told that if we "sincerely put [these maxims] into practice with order and discretion, [we] will discover in them great delight and consolation." So much for the death of appetite! Moreover, the "order and discretion" that should attend putting these rules into practice requires a context, and that is supplied by the "verses presented in *The Ascent of Mount Carmel*...which are instructions for climbing to the summit, the high state of union."[11] And even before they are repeated here, John reminds us that they "will here bear reference to the sensory part. Afterward, in the second division of this night, they may be interpreted in relationship to the spiritual part." By that time, the initial image of ourselves "climbing to the summit" will have been replaced by one of being led or drawn, as Dante was by his love for Beatrice.

Many will be familiar with the verses from T. S. Eliot's *Four Quartets,* where their inherently paradoxical character offers him the frame appropriate for a life responsive to grace.[12] In the words of John of the Cross:

> To reach satisfaction in all
> desire its possession in nothing.
> To come to possess all
> desire the possession of nothing.
> To arrive at being all
> desire to be nothing.
> To come to the knowledge of all
> desire the knowledge of nothing.

The spirit must be emptied out to dwell "in the center of its humility, [for] when it covets something, in this very desire it is wearied."[13] This is the sovereign freedom to which John hears the scriptures calling a faithful seeker. He endeavors to sketch out the way to attain it. Rigorous beginnings require unwelcome effort. In a disconcerting middle stage of darkness initiative is slowly shifted from the climbers to the One drawing them—from our efforts to God's activity in us. An ecstatic finale is best imaged as "the holy city, the new Jerusalem, coming down out of heaven from God, prepared as a bride dressed for her husband"

(Rv 21:2). In other words, the journey that John so carefully maps is tailored, as journeys have to be, to the end promised. The unwelcome dimensions of that journey mirror the destructive and often offensive accounts in the book of Revelation detailing the cataclysms presaging the end.

John of the Cross may have helped to answer our original question: Why so much violent destruction just before the end? What has to be destroyed is the entire ersatz world constructed by human pretension, a world of our own making that inhibits our access to and appreciation of the world created freely by God. Ironically, if God's world is created "from nothing," so is ours, but ours embodies the nothingness of our independent ambitions. John calls these "appetites," which, *as independent* of the creator's plan, can only be *sin*. And sin, as we have seen, creates a world resistant to being set aright, even by the actions of that very Wisdom whose person orders creation! So the reason that world must be destroyed for the new one to take possession is the very reason why "the Christ must suffer and so enter into his glory." Then what about the larger world of nature? It is hardly news that what humans do or fail to do with the *trust* offered to us profoundly affects the natural world. So the feedback from our failures exhibited in the natural world makes our sinfulness manifest. In fact, that destructive evidence constitutes an unmistakable sign of what human sin is and does. Just as we can fool ourselves endlessly regarding our well-being until our bodies assault us with an unforeseen illness, so the collective body that is our natural world serves to display prominently those consequences of our actions we characteristically try to suppress.

That is one way we can hear Paul's pregnant observation that "we are well aware that the whole creation, until this time, has been groaning in labor pains" (Rom 8:22). For he continues: "We too, who have the first fruits of the Spirit, even we are groaning inside ourselves, waiting with eagerness for our bodies to be set free." Yet that eagerness must translate into patience, for while "in hope, we already have salvation, [it is] in hope, not visibly present....But having this hope for what we cannot yet see, we are able to wait for it with persevering confidence" (8:24–25). John of the Cross has translated that waiting into an adventurous journey, employing a strategy that parallels the Sufi spiritual writing of Islam, whether consciously or subliminally. Paul had already sketched a picture of the Christian life that stressed its eschatological character: We have been made free but are not yet ourselves freed. That perspective links Christians with Jews as well: While we remain separated by our response to the claim that Jesus is the one whom the Lord promised to Moses—"I shall raise up a prophet like yourself" (Dt 18:18, cf. Jn 1:21), we are all challenged alike by the fear that when he comes we will fail to recognize him. Thus our avowal as Christians that Jesus indeed was the one who is to come in no way assures us that we would recognize him were he to make himself known in the midst of our world today. And the most we are told about his final coming, aside from the cataclysmic accompaniment, is that "the last shall be first, and the first last." And that disarmingly simple phrase may portend as much as the dramatic apocalyptic scenarios, for the promised coming notably promises to upset all of the arrangements on which we had come to count.

So the last word in biblical and Qur'anic revelation returns us to the present moment, presenting us with dramatic scenes designed to make us aware of our current situation. Many of them are lurid in their descriptive force yet they were never meant to be literally descriptive; apocalyptic is a genre all its own. It is so omnipresent in the Qur'an that the entire work shares in its fervor; the gospels and the prophetic writings also contain their share of it. Yet to read the accounts of Jesus' life and death or the historical books of the Bible in an apocalyptic perspective helps us to appreciate how peculiar are their own distinctive genres. For the purposes of our inquiry, we can now see how these apocalyptic tableaux of nature translate easily into critical moments of discernment, thanks especially to John of the Cross. However much human history has been intent on differentiating human nature from nature, Jewish and Christian scriptures, as well as the Qur'an, show them to be engaged in a shared drama. A poet such as John of the Cross, nourished by these traditions, discloses to us the relationships between nature and human nature, in the realms of both sin and grace.

9

EPILOGUE: DISCOVERING
THE ORIGINAL PEACE

Our leading image of doing theology elliptically, so that the twin foci of creation and redemption are jointly allowed to direct our exercise, offers an initial pattern for recasting our attempt to cast the Christian story. The various comparative exercises are designed to show the fruitfulness of these two centers—creation and redemption—mutually illuminating each other. Yet that image of foci remains a static one, useful though it may be in calling attention to the monocentric pattern that has dominated baroque Christian theology, while focusing it uniquely on Christology. We saw how that single focus allowed the second article of the baptismal creed to dominate. Seeking to restore the balance between the first and second articles, we implicitly relied on the third. We also came to realize how a comparative perspective, notably that of Islam, can contribute to keeping these two centers in a creative tension.

Yet balance too evokes a relatively static image for the issues with which we are concerned. A study by James Alison, which appeared while we were in the final redaction of these essays, brings these efforts of ours into a more dramatic, not to say dialectical, field of force, animated by the provocative work of René Girard.[1] James Alison's approach allows him to bring out something that our leading image left all too implicit, yet that has actually guided our reflections throughout. That is, that we can understand one of these poles, say, creation, only by reference to the other, and vice-versa. It is not as though we could have had a working grasp of creation, which our understanding of the redemptive activity of Jesus would then complete. Rather, the single-minded activity of Jesus, wholly intent on restoring God's original peace, is what leads us to appreciate the reaches of that original gift. That is, of course, what we have seen in John of the Cross, restoring the beauty of creation to us at the very end of his assiduous spiritual journey.

But let James Alison's own words round out our efforts:

[Jesus] was working to bring to existence what God had always wanted, but which had become trapped in the violent and fatal parody...which we tend to live out. So what Jesus was bringing into being was the fulfillment of creation, and this he knew very well he was doing. [So] the understanding of God as Creator changes from someone who once did something to someone who is doing something through Jesus, who was in on what the Father was doing through him from the beginning. Creation is not finished until Jesus dies (shouting *tetelestai*—it is accomplished), thus opening the whole of creation, which consequently begins fully, in a completely new way, in the garden on the first day of the week. [So] we understand creation starting from and through Jesus. God's graciousness, which brings what is not into existence from nothing, is exactly the same thing as Jesus' death-less self-giving out of love which enables him to break the human culture of death and is a self-giving which is entirely fixed on bringing into being a radiantly living and exuberant culture....The salvation which Jesus was working was, at the same time, the fulfillment of creation. This was the power and authority in Jesus' works and words and signs. Through him the Creator was bringing his work to completion.[2]

This extensive quotation will, we hope, whet those desires kindled by our efforts to continue the journey with James Alison to "recover the eschatological imagination," and so experience one of the ways the undertaking we have begun here can lead us further. Alison's ostensible guide is, as we have noted, René Girard, yet his pages will remind some readers of the surprises that lace the writings of Sebastian Moore.[3] For both Alison and Moore share a conviction that we have attempted to embody in these reflections: that the classical Christian message is ceaselessly capable of "subverting from within"—a favorite phrase of Alison as well as a constant practice of Moore—the ways in which we have allowed it to sediment. We have offered one strategy for uncovering our own myopia, to allow the message itself to resonate more fully; James Alison and Sebastian Moore suggest yet other tacks. Each is based on an analysis of how theological approaches may have covered over the very dynamic they were intended to feature. Therein lies one more humbling admonition to us theologians, especially those intent on "revising": Our efforts will inescapably be intent on correcting past missteps, as our successors will doubtless be busy amending ours. And that is the way it has to be, given our myopic grasp of God's revelation, but our efforts will not betray the community if their goal remains that of letting the message itself shine through, for the glory of God and the illumination of our brothers and sisters along the way.

We bring this book to a close at a point that is, we think, theologically appropriate. Yet the conclusion remains to be written, and that will doubtless be the work of others. The very logic of our argument for the necessity of positing creation and redemption as twin foci of Christian theology calls for a sustained exploration of resurrection. In the Christian perspective, faith in resurrection completes as it reveals the full meaning of both creation and redemption. For the end of God's process of restoring creation to its original peace is resurrection. Christian theology has always understood the doctrine of resurrection in cosmic as well as human dimensions, and resurrection for human beings in social as well as individual terms. The "new Jerusalem" in Revelation simultaneously represents the perfection of the created universe, the fulfillment of each redeemed person, and the realization of human community in all its cosmic, social, and personal relationships.

How could we better understand what resurrection means? How might we imagine the unimaginable promise of the Lord? We know, of course, that resurrection cannot be articulated adequately in human language any more than creation can. Yet is not that effort to find human words for the ineffable mysteries of God precisely what theology is all about? (James Alison has some wonderful reflections on the role of analogical understanding in the Catholic tradition.)[4] None of us can do it all, so our bequest is that someone else think through the implications of our work on creation and redemption for the light it casts on the doctrine of resurrection.

NOTES

INTRODUCTION: AN INTERFAITH APPROACH

1. Nicholas Lash, *Believing Three Ways in One God* (Notre Dame, Ind.: University of Notre Dame Press, 1993). John McDade, S.J. "Creation and Salvation: Green Faith and Christian Themes," *The Month* 23 (1990) 433–41.1.

1. HUMAN'S PLACE IN GOD'S CREATION

1. Thomas Michel, S.J., "God's Covenant with Mankind according to the Qur'an," *Bulletin* [Secretariatus pro non-Christianis—Vatican] 18 (1983): 41.

2. Fazlur Rahman, *Major Themes of the Qur'an* (Chicago: Bibliotheca Islamica, 1980), p. 9.

3. Those interested in an ampler treatment of this theme will be rewarded by consulting ibid., chap. 1, esp. p. 15.

4. Eric L. Ormsby, "Creation in Time in Islamic Thought with Special Reference to al-Ghazâlî," in *God and Creation: An Ecumenical Symposium,* eds. David Burrell and Bernard McGinn (Notre Dame, Ind.: University of Notre Dame Press, 1990), p. 261.

5. Cf. *Al-Ghazâlî on the Nintey-Nine Beautiful Names of God,* trans. David Burrell and Nazih Daher (Cambridge: Islamic Texts Society, 1992): *ar-Rahman* [The Compassionate] 52–57, *al-'Adl* [The Just] 92–96, *al-Karîm* [The Generous] 113–14.

2. THE MISSION OF JESUS

1. John Milbank, *Theology and Social Theory* (Oxford: Blackwell, 1993), pp. 417, 430–32.

2. The phrase has recently been exploited by René Girard as the title of an extended dialogic essay exploring his thesis on the origins of violence in the world: *Les choses cachés depuis la fondation du monde* (Paris: Grasset, 1978); English trans. by Stephen Bann and Michael Metteer, *Things Hidden from the Foundation of theWorld* (London: Athlone, 1987).

3. Herbert Fingarette, *Self-Deception* (New York: Humanities Press, 1969); for a theological reading, see David Burrell and Stanley Hauerwas, "Autobiography and Self-Deception: Theological and Ethical Reflections on Albert Speer's *Inside the Third Reich,*" *Journal of Reliigous Ethics* 2 (1974): 99–117.

4. Bernard J. F. Lonergan, *Grace and Freedom: Operative Grace in the Thought of St. Thomas Aquinas* (London: Darton, Longman and Todd, 1971), pp. 111–14.

5. Augustine, *Confessions,* esp. Book 8. See the discussion of Jung's antipathy to this position in David Burrell, *Exercises in Religious Understanding* (Notre Dame, Ind.: University of Notre Dame Press, 1974), chap. 5 ("Jung: A Language for Soul").

6. The statement of Jesus' crucifixion as atonement that avoids the many pitfalls of classical formulations is Sebastian Moore's contemporary classic, *The Crucified Jesus Is no Stranger* (New York: Paulist, 1993).

7. The commentator whose prose seems best to match the realities involved is certainly Susan George; see her *How the Other Half Dies* (London: Penguin, 1976) and *A Fate Worse than Debt* (London: Penguin, 1988).

8. Peter Winch, "Towards Understanding a Primitive Society," in *Religion and Understanding,* ed., D. Z. Phillips (Oxford: Blackwell, 1967), pp. 9–42.

9. For a current study of this dimension of ecclesial life and practice, see Laurence F. X. Brett, *Redeemed Creation: Sacramentals Today* (Wilmington, Del.: Michael Glazier, 1984).

10. Perhaps the most substantive of these writers is Thomas Berry, whose "The New Story" appeared in *Teilhard Studies* (1978): 1–13.

11. To trace this trajectory in Islamic thought, see David Burrell, *Freedom and Creation in Three Traditions* (Notre Dame, Ind.: University of Notre Dame Press, 1993). We are indebted to Nicholas Lash for the observation about culture in his *Believing Three Ways in One God.*

12. Kathryn Tanner's *God and the Doctrine of Creation* (New York: Blackwell, 1990) develops this point nicely.

13. We shall always remain indebted to Bernard J. F. Lonergan for reminding us of the original intent of the natural/supernatural distinction. See his *Grace and Freeedom,* pp. 13–19.

3. WHY "THE CHRIST MUST SUFFER..."

1. Aquinas responds to the charge that there is more evil than good in the universe by distinguishing the world of nature from the human domain. Only in the latter does "evil, for the most part, prevail" (*Summa Theologiae,* 1.49.3.5). Given the dominance of knowledge as power, however, it has become increasingly difficult to sustain his crucial distinction.

2. Nicholas Lash, in his *A Matter of Hope* (Notre Dame, Ind.: University of Notre Dame Press, 1982), offers an illuminating distinction between *hope* and *optimism.*

3. For René Girard, see his *The Scapegoat,* trans. Yvonne Freccero (Baltimore: Johns Hopkins University Press, 1986), and for a comprehensive bibliography of his work, see *To Honor René Girard* (Saratoga, CA: Anima Libri, 1986).

4. Translations of the *Confessions* abound; the two most recent are by R. S. Pine-Coffin (Penguin) and Henry Chadwick (Oxford), while Hackett (Indianapolis) has reissued Frank Sheed's most readable text with an introduction by Peter Brown. (References will be by book and chapter.) We are indebted to two colleagues, John Cavadini and James Wetzel, for continuing to instruct us about Augustine.

4. HUMAN DEATH, HUMAN SUFFERING

1. John McDade, "Creation and Salvation: Green Faith and Christian Themes," *The Month* 23 (1990): 438. The emphasis on martyrdom in John Paul II's *Veritatis Splendor* is telling in this regard.

2. Notably Schubert Ogden, *The Reality of God* (New York: Harper, 1963), chap. 8 ("The Promise of Faith").

3. For Islam, see Margaret Smith, *Râbi'a the Mystic and Her Fellow Saints in Islam* (Cambridge: Cambridge University Press, 1928/1984); for Christianity, see the autobiography of Thérèse of Lisieux, *Story of a Soul* (Washington, D.C.: Institute of Carmelite Studies, 1976).

4. Herbert Mason, *Gilgamesh: A Verse Narrative* (New York: Penguin, 1972).

5. Ernest Becker, *Denial of Death* (New York: Free Press, 1973).

6. Ibid.

7. Kathryn Tanner, *God and the Doctrine of Creation;* also Aquinas: "*esse* is innermost in each thing" (ST 1.8.1).

8. For an enlightening comparison of Buddhism and Christianity, see Carrin Dunne's lasting little volume *Buddha and Jesus: Conversations* (Springfield, Ill.: Templegate Press, 1975).

5. THE ECONOMY OF THE SACRAMENTS

1. While it is risky to single out one book from so many, a sterling example would be Sandra DeGidio's *Sacraments Alive* (Mystic, Conn.: Twenty-Third Publications, 1991).

2. Louis-Marie Chauvet in *Symbole et Sacrement* (Paris: Cerf, 1988), accomplishes this task masterfully.

3. See David Power's *Pastoral Care of the Sick* (Philadelphia: Trinity Press International, 1992).

4. Karl Menninger, *Whatever Became of Sin?* (New York: Hawthorne, 1973).

5. See William Moyers's recent television series, published as *Healing and the Mind* (New York: Doubleday, 1993).

6. Peter Winch: "On Understanding a Primitive Society," in *Religion*

and Understanding, ed. D. Z. Phillips (Oxford: Blackwell, 1967), pp. 9–42.

7. Ernest Becker, *The Denial of Death* (New York: Free Press, 1973).

8. For an ecumenical perspective, see Dennis Hughes, "Anointing and Prayers for Restoration of the Sick: Reclaiming a Biblical Mandate," *Reformed Liturgy and Music* 24 (1990): 136–39.

9. And while this is clear in the biblical text, it is telling that both Jewish and Christian exegesis will locate the divine image in the human intellect and will. This alteration can certainly be traced to the influences of Hellenic philosophy, yet there may be other factors at work as well.

10. The work of Michel Foucault has sketched out in one context after another how "heirarchical" orderings tend to reinforce power dominations; for a summary, see Gary Gutting, *Michel Foucault's Archaeology of Scientific Reason* (Cambridge: Cambridge University Press, 1989).

11. For this final challenge to our remarkably unreflective American contemporaries in ecclesiology, as well as for the observation about Donatism, we are indebted to conversations over the years with our colleague Stanley Hauerwas, conversations that have invariably stiumulated us to further thought on these matters. Donatism needs to be specified: The efficaciousness of the sacramental action was tied to the personal holiness of the minister; the proper understanding of the contrary formula *ex opere operato* is not that the minister's personal holiness is irrelevant but that the church is the primary agent in all the sacraments.

6. A WAY TO RESTORE CREATION

1. Henri deLubac's *Surnaturel* was researched during the Second World War and published immediately afterward, sounding a clarion call for the "nouvelle théologie" movement (English translation: *The Mystery of the Supernatural* [New York: Herder, 1967]).

2. Michael Buckley has shown how a hard and fast distinction, if not separation of philosophy from theology, marked baroque Catholic thought: *At the Origins of Modern Atheism* (New Haven: Yale University Press, 1987).

3. The term suggests the sense in which an atheistic account is parasitic upon theological perspectives, as the very term *a-theism* indicates.

4. For an overview of Milbank's formidable book, see David Burrell, "An Introduction to *Theology and Social Theory,*" *Modern Theology* 8 (1992): 319–30.

5. These untoward and certainly unforeseen consequences may be added to those discerned by Buckley in his *Origins of Modern Atheism.*

6. Ewert Cousins, *Christ of the 21st Century* (Rockport, Mass.: Element, 1992), p. 113.

7. Ibid. He explicitly acknowledges John S. Dunne, C.S.C., for the simple yet pregnant metaphor of "passing over and returning" as a principal method in comparative religious understanding.

8. See J. A. DiNoia, O.P., *Diversity of Religions* (Washington, D.C.: Catholic University of America Press, 1993), for a trenchant critique of such "soteriocentric" approaches, and a daring effort to recast the discussion in terms well beyond the tired and unilluminating *inclusive/exclusive/pluralist* typology.

9. For an engaging introduction to Sufi thought in English see Annemarie Schimmel, *Mystical Dimensions of Islam* (Chapel Hill: University of North Carolina Press, 1975).

10. See Roger Arnaldez, *Three Messengers for One God,* trans. Gerald Schlabach et al. (Notre Dame, Ind.: University of Notre Dame Press, 1994); also Paul Wadell, *The Primacy of Love* (New York: Paulist, 1992).

11. Sebastian Moore, *The Crucified Jesus Is No Stranger* (New York: Crossroad, 1980/Paulist, 1992).

12. Robert Sokolowski, *God of Faith and Reason* (Notre Dame, Ind.: University of Notre Dame Press, 1983), *passim.*

13. For a fascinating account of the historical and conceptual wrangles leading up to Chalcedon, see Thomas Weinandy, *Does God Change?* (Still River, Mass.: St. Bede's Publications, 1985).

14. See David Burrell, *Knowing the Unknowable God: Ibn Sina, Maimonides, Aquinas* (Notre Dame, Ind.: University of Notre Dame Press, 1986) for an extended narrative and account of this interfaith drama, continued in *Freedom and Creation in Three Traditions* (Notre Dame, Ind.: University of Notre Dame Press, 1993).

15. Kathryn Tanner, *God and the Doctrine of Creation* (New York: Blackwell, 1990), presents a sustained argument against this propensity.

16. For al-Hllaj, see Herbert Mason, *Hallâj: Mystic and Martyr* (Princeton, N.J.: Princeton University Press, 1994; abridged ed.); and for Ibn al-Arabi, William Chittick, *The Sufi Path of Kowledge* (Albany: SUNY Press, 1989).

17. Indeed, the reduplication in the phrase "on account of the love of His own goodness" would seem to be deliberate, in order to avoid even the hint of a neoplatonic constraint whereby *good* is said to be "diffusive by its very nature." See *Freedom and Creation*, pp. 165–66.

7. THE CREATOR AND CREATION

1. Kathryn Tanner, *God and the Doctrine of Creation.*

2. Sara Grant has lived since 1972 in an interfaith ashram in Pune in India, Christa Prema Seva Ashram. Her slim volume presents the Teape lectures offered at Cambridge in 1989. *Towards an Alternative Theology: Confessions of a Non-dualist Christian* (Bangalore, India: Asian Trading Corporation, 1991), available from the Asian Trading Corporation, 150 Brigade Road, Bangalore 560 025, India.

3. Ibid., p. 48.

4. Ibid., p. 18.

5. Ibid., p. 17.

6. Correlating "relation" with "distinction" can align this treatment with that of Robert Sokolowski in *The God of Faith and Reason* (Notre Dame, Ind.: University of Notre Dame Press, 1981).

7. For a brief discussion of the Mu'tazilite position in Islamic philosophical theology, see my *Freedom and Creation in Three Traditions*, pp. 51–53, 77–79.

8. Ibid., p. 17.

9. Ibid., p. 28.

10. L. Krempel, *La doctrine de la Rélation chez Saint Thomas* (Paris: J. Vrin, 1952).

11. Ibid., p. 49.

12. Ibid., p. 48.

13. See James Ross, "Creation II," in Alfredo Freddoso, *The Existence*

and Nature of God, (Notre Dame, Ind.: University of Notre Dame Press, 1983), pp. 115–42, esp. 127.

14. Grant, *Towards an Alternative Theology,* p. 49.

15. Ibid., p. 77.

16. Ibid., p. 77. The title of a fine presentation of the church's torturous path to the Chalcedonian formula plays on the ambiguity of the faith-phrase "God became man"; see Thomas Weinandy, *Does God Change?* (Still River, Mass.: St. Bede's Publications, 1989).

17. Ibid., p. 75.

8. THE END OF IT ALL

1. References will be to the *Collected Works of St. John of the Cross,* translated by Kieran Kavanaugh, O.C.D., and Otilio Rodriguez, O.C.D. (Washington D.C.: Institute of Carmelite Studies, 1975).

2. See Sebastian Moore, *Jesus the Liberator of Desire* (New York: Crossroad, 1989).

3. This is the burden of the early chapters of the *Ascent of Mount Carmel,* notably Book 1, ch. 13.

4. John of the Cross, *Collected Works,* p. 557.

5. Ibid., p. 561.

6. Translated by Howard Yoder and Elmer Douglas (New York: Vantage Press, 1981), first published as *Un Precursor Hispano-Musulman de San Juan de la Cruz* (Madrid: Al-Andalus 1, 1933).

7. Nadjm Oud-Dine Bammate, "Freedom according to Islam," in *Christianity and Freedom: A Symposium* (New York: Philosophical Library, 1956), 34–50, citation at p. 37.

8. Ibid., pp. 41–42.

9. Ibid., p. 48.

10. Book 1, ch. 13, p. 102.

11. Ibid., p. 103.

12. T. S. Eliot, *Four Quartets* (New York: Harcourt Brace Jovanovich, 1971): "East Coker," lines 130–46; pp. 28–29.

13. John of the Cross, *Collected Works,* p. 103.

9. DISCOVERING THE ORIGINAL PEACE

1. James Alison, *Raising Abel: The Recovery of the Eschatological Imagination* (New York: Crossroad, 1966), p. 55; the most relevant source of Girard's is *Things Hidden from the Foundation of the World,* trans. Stephen Bann and Michael Metteer (London: Athlone, 1987).

2. Alison, *Raising Abel,* p. 55.

3. Among the works of Sebastian Moore that we have in mind are *The Crucified Jesus Is No Stranger* (New York: Crossroad, 1980/Paulist, 1992); *The Fire and the Rose Are One* (New York: Seabury, 1980); and *Jesus the Liberator of Desire* (New York: Crossroad, 1989).

4. Alison, *Raising Abel,* pp. 67–69.